Best
Practices
for
High
School
Classrooms

More Books by Randi Stone

MORE Best Practices for Middle School Classrooms: What Award-Winning Teachers Do, 2010

MORE Best Practices for Elementary Classrooms: What Award-Winning Teachers Do, 2009

Best Practices for Teaching Reading: What Award-Winning Classroom Teachers Do, 2008

Best Practices for Teaching Social Studies: What Award-Winning Classroom Teachers Do, 2008

Best Practices for Teaching Writing: What Award-Winning Classroom Teachers Do, 2007

Best Practices for Teaching Mathematics: What Award-Winning Classroom Teachers Do, 2007

Best Practices for Teaching Science: What Award-Winning Classroom Teachers Do, 2007

Best Classroom Management Practices for Reaching All Learners: What Award-Winning Classroom Teachers Do, 2005

Best Teaching Practices for Reaching All Learners: What Award-Winning Classroom Teachers Do, 2004

What?! Another New Mandate? What Award-Winning Teachers Do When School Rules Change, 2002

Best Practices for High School Classrooms: What Award-Winning Secondary Teachers Do, 2001

Best Classroom Practices: What Award-Winning Elementary Teachers Do, 1999

New Ways to Teach Using Cable Television: A Step-by-Step Guide, 1997

Best Practices for High School Classrooms

What Award-Winning Secondary Teachers Do

RANDI STONE

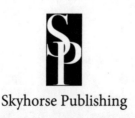

Skyhorse Publishing

Skyhorse Publishing books may be purchased in bulk at special discounts for sales promotion, corporate gifts, fund-raising, or educational purposes. Special editions can also be created to specifications. For details, contact the Special Sales Department, Skyhorse Publishing, 307 West 36th Street, 11th Floor, New York, NY 10018 or info@skyhorsepublishing.com.

Skyhorse® and Skyhorse Publishing® are registered trademarks of Skyhorse Publishing, Inc.®, a Delaware corporation.

Visit our website at www.skyhorsepublishing.com.

10 9 8 7 6 5 4 3 2 1

Library of Congress Cataloging-in-Publication Data is available on file.

Cover design by Michael Dubowe

Print ISBN: 978-1-63220-543-8
Ebook ISBN: 978-1-63220-960-3

Printed in the United States of America

Contents

Preface

My goal of helping teachers benefit from each others' great ideas has remained the same for over a decade. These are the teachers we read about in journals and magazines, the teachers who win grants, fellowships, and contests; they are the recipients of awards from Time Warner Cable, NCTE, the U.S. and state Departments of Education, the Milken Foundation, NSTA, ASCD, and the Herb Kohl Educational Foundation, among many others.

There is endless information out there and it can take hours to find just what you are seeking. This book makes it easy to find what you need. Within the four parts (Classroom Practices Across the Curriculum; Teaching Science and Math; Teaching Language Arts and Social Studies; and Teaching Music, Art, and Physical Education) are chapters with such varied titles as "Nine Co-Teaching Tips from Two Co-Teaching Gurus," "Video Analysis Unlocks the Physics World," "Parabolic Solar Cooker," "Take Me Out to the Ball Game: Building Sentence Sense Without Teaching Grammar," "Navigating *Spoon River* While Putting Your Students in the Spotlight," "Economics in My Hometown," and "Creating Correct Vowels for Singing."

I hope you enjoy each submission with the same enthusiasm and excitement that I did as I chose these innovative lessons from among the many offered by the generous secondary educators who responded to the invitation to contribute to this new volume. Who wouldn't enjoy "poking their nose" into classrooms like these?

Acknowledgments

We gratefully acknowledges the contribution of the following reviews:

Melody L. Aldrich
Teacher
Florence High School
Florence, Arizona

Dr. Judy Butler
Associate Professor of Education
University of West Georgia
Carrollton, Georgia

David Freitas, EdD
Professor
Indiana University South Bend
South Bend, Indiana

Janice L. Hall
Retired Associate Professor of Education

Linda D. Jungwirth, EdD
President, Convening Conversations
Adjunct Professor
Educational Administration, Leadership,
   and Policy Doctoral Program
Pepperdine University
Redlands, California

About the Author

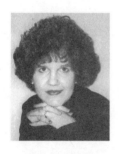 **Randi Stone** is a graduate of Clark University, Boston University, and Salem State College. She completed her doctorate in education at the University of Massachusetts, Lowell. She is the author of numerous books, including her series *Best Practices for Teaching Reading: What Award-Winning Teachers Do, Best Practices for Teaching Writing: What Award-Winning Teachers Do, Best Practices for Teaching Mathematics: What Award-Winning Teachers Do, Best Practices for Teaching Science: What Award-Winning Teachers Do,* and *Best Practices for Teaching Mathematics: What Award-Winning Teachers Do.* She lives with her teenage daughter, Blair, in Keene, New Hampshire.

About the Contributors

Fonda Akins, Special Education Teacher, Springfield High School, Springfield, Pennsylvania
> E-mail: fondaakins@rcn.com

> *Number of years teaching:* 16

Terry Armstrong, Social Studies Teacher, Lordstown High School, Warren, Ohio
> E-mail: terry.armstrong@neomin.org

> *Number of years teaching:* 3
> *Award:* Time Warner Cable National Teacher Award, 2008

Spencer Arnaud, English Teacher, Beau Chêne High School, Arnaudville, Louisiana
> E-mail: sca2624@slp.k12.la.us

> *Number of years teaching:* 15
> *Awards:* Beau Chêne High School Teacher of the Year, 2008–2009; ING Unsung Heroes Award for Innovative Teaching, 2008–2009; National Board Certification, 2004–2005

Judy Osburn Beemer, Literacy Coach, Junction City High School, Junction City, Kansas
> E-mail: judybeemer@usd475.org

> *Number of years teaching:* 33
> *Awards:* National Council of Teachers of English Secondary Teacher of Excellence, 2008; Unified School District #475 Teacher of the Year Award, 2007; Kansas Teacher of the Year Finalist, 1997

Robert Benway, Physics Teacher, James River High School, Midlothian, Virginia

E-mail: Robert_Benway@ccpsnet.net

Number of years teaching: 5

Awards: Recipient of Teaching Excellence Award from Virginia's Department of Education, 2005; Recipient of New Teacher of the Year for Henrico County, 2004

Suzanne Blair, Mathematics Teacher, Gardner Edgerton High School, Gardner, Kansas

E-mail: blairs@usd231.com

Number of years teaching: 17

Awards: American Star of Teaching, 2008 (U.S. Department of Education); Claes Nobel Educator of Distinction, 2007 (National Society of High School Scholars); Teacher of the Year, 2007 (Gardner Edgerton Unified School District #231)

Christina M. Charles, Biology Teacher, Deerfield High School, Deerfield, Wisconsin

E-mail: charlesc@deerfield.k12.wi.us

Number of years teaching: 3

Awards: New Science Teacher Academy Fellow, National Science Teacher Association-Amgen, 2009; Distinguished Educator Award, Nutrients for Life Foundation, 2008; Maitland P. Simmons New Teacher Award, National Science Teacher Association, 2007

Cindy Couchman, Math Instructor and Department Chair, Buhler High School, Buhler, Kansas

E-mail: ccouchman@buhlerschools.org

Number of years teaching: 19

Awards: Kansas Teacher of the Year, 2009; Presidential Award for Excellence in Mathematics and Science Teaching State Finalist, 2008; National Board Certified Teacher, Adolescent and Young Adulthood Mathematics, 2006

Timothy Couillard, Physics Teacher, James River High School, Midlothian, Virginia

E-mail: timothy_couillard@ccpsnet.net

Number of years teaching: 13

Awards: Recipient of the National Science Teacher Association/ CIBA Foundation Exemplary High School Teaching Award, 2009; 3rd Place Recipient, Air Force Association National Teacher of the Year Award, 2008; Recipient of the National Science Teacher Association/Vernier Technology Award, 2007

Cindy Armitage Dannaker, English Teacher, E. T. Richardson Middle School, Springfield, Pennsylvania

E-mail: dannacin@ssd.k12.pa.us

Number of years teaching: 22

Awards: Snag-in-the-River Award, Delaware Valley Region Pennsylvania Association of Supervision and Curriculum Development for Excellence in Teaching, 2008; Education Department Outstanding Service Award, Villanova University, Villanova, Pennsylvania, 2005; Outstanding Teacher Award (nominated by a Springfield High School student), Denison University, Ohio, 2001

Alicia Deel, Special Education Teacher, Grundy High School, Grundy, Virginia

E-mail: adeel@buc.k12.va.us

Number of years teaching: 10

Awards: National Association of Special Education Teachers' Outstanding Special Education Teacher Award, 2008; Who's Who Among High School Teachers, 2007; American Legion Teacher of the Year, 2006

Chris Dodds, Industrial Technology Instructor, McClain High School, Greenfield, Ohio

Email: chrisandcheld@aol.com

Number of years teaching: 14
Awards: Time Warner Cable National Teacher Award—Teacher of the
        Year, 2008; Wal-Mart Teacher of the Year—Washington
        Court House, Ohio, 2006; Coach of the National Champion
        Hasbro/Sally Ride National Toy Challenge Competition, 2004

Kathleen Donaldson, Physical Education Teacher, Edgewood High
School, Edgewood, Maryland
    E-mail: Kathleen.Donaldson@hcps.org

Number of years teaching: 10
Awards: Simon McNeely Award, 2008; Softball Coach of the Year,
        2003

Keith Farnsworth, Art Teacher, Jerome High School, Jerome, Idaho
    E-mail: farnswork@d261.k12.id.us

Number of years teaching: 20
Award: Idaho's Art Teacher of the Year, 2008

Elizabeth G. Lutz-Hackett, English Teacher, Yellow Springs High
School, Yellow Springs, Ohio
    E-mail: yshs_elutz@k12server.mveca.org

Number of years teaching: 14
Awards: U.S. Department of Education American Star of Teaching
        Award, 2008; The Howard Post Excellence in Education
        Award, 2005, 2007, 2008; The Golden Apple Achiever Award,
        1998

Amy Maxey, Math Teacher, West Forsyth High School, Clemmons,
North Carolina
    E-mail: amaxey@wsfcs.k12.nc.us

Number of years teaching: 14
Awards: American Star of Teaching/U.S. Department of Education,
        2008; National Board Certification/AYA Mathematics, 2008;
        Winston-Salem Forsyth County Teacher of the Year, 2008

J-Petrina McCarty-Puhl, Secondary Science Teacher, Robert McQueen High School, Reno, Nevada; President, Nevada State Science Teachers Association
E-mail: pmccarty@washoe.k12.nv.us

Number of years teaching: 22
Awards: Nevada State Teacher of the Year, 2006; AOL-NEA Foundation Technology Leadership Award; Finalist, Shell Science Teaching Award, 2008

Kristen S. McDaniel, Economics Teacher and Social Studies Department Chair, Fort Atkinson High School, Fort Atkinson, Wisconsin
E-mail: mcdaniel@mail.fortschools.org

Number of years teaching: 13
Awards: Excellence in Teaching Economics and Financial Literacy Award, Second Place, 2008; NASDAQ National Teaching Award, Regional Semi-Finalist for the Midwest, 2005

Shane McKay, Anatomy/Physiology Teacher and Science Department Chair, East Central High School, San Antonio, Texas
E-mail: shane.mckay@fc.ecisd.net

Number of years teaching: 10
Awards: ING Unsung Hero Award, 2008; East Central ISD Teacher of the Year, 2008; East Central High School Teacher of the Year, 2008

Ken Petersen, Math Teacher, Mountain View High School, Mountain View, Wyoming
E-mail: petersenk@po.uinta4.k12.wy.us

Number of years teaching: 10
Awards: Presidential Awardee for Mathematics and Science Teaching, 2007; Uinta County School District Number 4 Teacher of the Year, 2005; Uinta County School District Number 4 Teacher of the Year, 2004

Jill Pinard, English Teacher, John Stark Regional High School, Weare, New Hampshire
E-mail: j_pinard@jsrhs.net

Number of years teaching: 16
Awards: Named 1 of 25 National Teachers of Excellence by the Secondary Section of the National Council of Teachers of English, 2008; Recognized at National Council of Teachers of English's Annual Convention, 2008; New Hampshire English Teacher of the Year, 2008; Selected by the New Hampshire Council of Teachers of English (NHCTE); Recognized at the NHCTE Spring Conference, 2008; Recognized at the New Hampshire Excellence in Education Awards (EDies), 2008

Christine Roland, Science Teacher, Edgewood High School, Edgewood, Maryland
E-mail: Christine.Roland@hcps.org

Number of years teaching: 7
Awards: Air Force Association Maryland State Teacher of the Year, 2008–2009; Harford County Teacher of the Year, 2007–2008

Ann E. Scharfenberg, Economics Teacher, New Richmond High School, New Richmond, Wisconsin
E-mail: anns@newrichmond.k12.wi.us

Number of years teaching: 15
Awards: Wisconsin Distinguished Teacher of the Year, awarded by Wisconsin Council for the Social Studies, 2009; Kohl Teacher Fellowship recipient awarded by Herb Kohl Educational Foundation, 2009; Excellence in Teaching Economics and Personal Finance, 3rd place senior division, awarded by Economics Wisconsin, 2007

Stan Scott, Vocal Music Instructor, Central High School, Grand Junction, Colorado
E-mail: sscott@mesa.k12.co.us

Number of years teaching: 24

Awards: Boettcher Foundation Teacher Recognition, 2006; Grand Junction Chamber of Commerce Teacher of the Year, 2003; Recognized as One of the Top Ten Music Educators in the State of Colorado by *Music Educators National Conference Magazine,* 2000

Ann Shioji, Science/AVID Teacher, Yerba Buena High School, San Jose, California

E-mail: ashioji@hotmail.com

Number of years teaching: 6

Awards: Delta/Frey/CPO Award for Excellence in Inquiry-Based Science Teaching, 2008; City of Los Angeles Most Inspirational Teacher Award, 2006; California Governor's Scholar, 2002

Justin G. Singleton, World Geography, Psychology, and Sociology Teacher, George W. Carver Magnet High School, Houston, Texas

E-mail: jsingleton@aldine.k12.tx.us

Number of years teaching: 8

Awards: Milken National Educator Award, 2007; KPRC Channel Two News Teacher of the Month, 2006; Carver Magnet High School Teacher of the Year, 2005

Gretchen Smith, Social Studies Teacher and Department Leader, North Hagerstown High School, Hagerstown, Maryland

E-mail: smithgre@wcboe.k12.md.us

Number of years teaching: 11

Award: Washington County Public Schools Teacher of the Year Finalist, 2008

Michelle L. Smith, Special Education Teacher, Palestine High School, Palestine, Illinois

E-mail: mlsmith47591@yahoo.com

Number of years teaching: 6

Award: Outstanding Special Education Teacher Award from the National Association of Special Education Teachers, 2007–2008

Rebecca Snyder, Secondary Language Arts Teacher and Department Head, Greater Latrobe Senior High School, Latrobe, Pennsylvania
E-mail: rebecca.snyder@glsd.k12.pa.us

Number of years teaching: 12

Awards: Pennsylvania Teacher of the Year, 2009; Cambridge Who's Who Among Business and Professional Women, 2007; National Honor Roll's Outstanding American Teacher, 2006

Carla Thompson, Physical Education and Health Teacher, Lakes Community High School, Lake Villa, Illinois
E-mail: cthompson@lakeseagles.com

Number of years teaching: 28

Awards: Illinois Association of Health, Physical Education, Recreation and Dance Teacher of the Year, 2007; North East District Illinois Association of Health, Physical Education, Recreation and Dance, Teacher of the Year, 2007; Suburban Department Chairman Association, Outstanding Teacher, 2007

Jeffery R. Wehr, Science Educator, Odessa High School, Odessa, Washington
E-mail: WehrdScience@yahoo.com or WehrJ@odessa.wednet.edu

Number of years teaching: 11

Awards: Department of Education American Star of Teaching Award: State of Washington, 2008; Regional Science Director Dedication and Service Award; Montana Science Teachers Association, 2004; Distinguished Service to Science Education Award, Montana Science Teachers Association, 2003

PART I

Classroom Practices Across the Curriculum

Classroom Management and Co-Teaching

Overview, Chapters 1–3

1. **Christina M. Charles**, a biology teacher in Deerfield, Wisconsin, shares guiding principles that put classroom management in perspective.

2. **Michelle L. Smith**, a special education teacher in Palestine, Illinois, encourages teachers to discover their own style of classroom management and offers some suggested guidance.

3. **Fonda Akins**, a special education teacher, and **Cindy Armitage Dannaker**, an English teacher, both in Springfield, Pennsylvania, present useful tips for co-teaching in an inclusion classroom.

▨ 1. Classroom Management: Ideas I've Picked Up Along the Way

Christina M. Charles
Deerfield, Wisconsin

Recommended Level: Grades 9–12

Overall Objective: Teachers can understand their goals and purpose by reflecting on these 12 guiding principles.

When I started teaching, I was really concerned about having control of my classroom. I truly felt like I had none and that the students were walking all over me—and definitely not learning much. My ideas have evolved as I have gained experience. Now, in my third year, I have developed some guiding principles that I use to examine how things are going in my classroom, and I want to share these with you.

1. **Understand your limits—which student behaviors bother you and what you are OK with.** People have different levels of tolerance. Be comfortable with yours and understand why you have those expectations. Keep reflecting on those expectations to see if they are helpful or need to be adjusted.

2. **Be yourself—be human.** Forget the "I am above you" attitude—students can see right through that. They don't want a person who they feel is going to judge them or make them feel inferior. They want a safe place to learn and grow.

3. **Understand and believe that what you are doing is important.** This one seems obvious, but in order for the students to believe in you, you have to believe in yourself. Sometimes this seems impossible, but going back to that belief will spare you from getting too down on yourself when things don't go as planned.

4. **Make an honest effort to get to know the students—who they are, what they are about, and what makes them tick.** This will give you a context for working with them and help you to engage in meaningful interactions. It will help you to understand the reasons for their actions, especially when they do something that bothers you.

5. **Understand and believe that every student has something to offer.** Students appreciate this so much! What person doesn't want to feel like they can contribute somehow? Being able to find ways to bring everyone to the table is a talent that can be honed, and it works! If people feel great about what they have to offer, they are less likely to act out and more likely to take healthy learning risks.

6. **Get to the bottom of behavioral situations—go beyond the symptoms.** Very few people wake up and say to themselves, "I really want to get in trouble today. I want to make someone's day miserable." Things happen, and there is usually some reason. Try to get to the bottom of the problem, instead of getting upset yourself. Don't make assumptions. Try to ask yourself, "Why is this student acting this way?" Even ask them! A simple, "Are you OK?" goes a long way.

7. **Put yourself in their shoes—this is not about you or your curriculum. This is about their trying to make sense of their impending adulthood.** Sometimes I get so caught up in what I'm trying to accomplish as a teacher, I forget that this is mostly their journey. They have so many other day-to-day things going on. Teaching in a high school, I observe teenage drama all the time. Most often, the drama is much more important to them than their biology curriculum. So take it in stride, and remember when you were in high school—you probably felt the same way!

8. **Make your classroom a safe place to explore, grow, and learn.** Learning is not easy. We all have to struggle a bit with new material at some point. The important thing for students to understand is that this is a part of the process; they have a hard time believing this! They have to feel safe to struggle, to be wrong, to ask every question they can think of, to be interested, to open their minds. I always tell them, "If you already knew this stuff, I'd be out of a job!"

9. **Make students part of the decision-making process.** At the beginning of the year, I like to establish guidelines with the students. Allowing them to give input helps them to realize that the classroom is theirs and that they have a stake in how it goes. It's also a good way to take issues to them if things are not going smoothly. I ask, "What happened? How could we have done things differently? What will we do next time?" Or when they complain about something, "What ideas do you have? How would you like this to proceed?"

10. **Understand that *control*, in the conventional sense, is an illusion—this is not a school for compliant robots, but for young people who are trying to figure out who they are.** Humans belong to the species *Homo sapiens*. This translates, more or less, to *wise man*. Along with this wisdom comes free thought. And people who have the capacity to think for themselves will not be controlled easily. Think about it—what do you want for your students anyway? Do you want to teach them to sit down and shut up or to use their unique voices and talents to make the world a better place? Helping students hone critical thinking skills, as opposed to trying to suppress or control them, will help them to become better, more capable adults.

11. **Try to treat every day like a new one—students really appreciate a clean slate, and you will fare much better for it yourself.** Don't hang on to the past. It's a waste of your energy, and students, like anyone else, can sense resentment or dislike. How would you feel if you made a mistake in the classroom and had to pay for it every day? Would you want to be there? Would you bother to try after a while? Try to think of what you would want from other people if you were the one under fire; then use that approach with students.

12. **Try to put yourself in parents' shoes.** If you were the parent of these students, what would you want for them? What would you see in them? What would you expect of the students' teachers? This principle really helps me to do my best for the students and to hold on to my standards.

Finally, I want to note that these are guiding principles. Like everyone else, I have good and bad days—when I forget these principles or, just like the students, wish I had done better! Making a conscious effort will go a long way toward things getting better. Also, I encourage you to question the entire premise of "classroom management." What does it mean to "manage" people? Can people be managed? Do your goals as a teacher involve students doing everything you ask or listening to everything you say? If so, maybe the conventional, behaviorist management approach is best for you. But if you want your students to enjoy and make the most of their learning (about school subjects, themselves, and others), then maybe controlling behavior just won't cut it. Conscientiously observing these principles or developing your own set of guidelines could go a long way in developing respectful, courteous, lifelong learners.

As an additional note, many of my ideas have been greatly influenced by the fantastic Alfie Kohn. I encourage anyone who wants to learn more about student empowerment and community to read his books.

2. Teenagers and Rules and Learning . . . Oh My!

Michelle L. Smith
Palestine, Illinois

Recommended Level: Grades 9–12

Overall Objective: Teachers can discover their own style of classroom management and make it work, whether they are in a general or special education classroom.

The thought of standing in front of a group of hormone-crazed teenagers without reinforcements can strike fear in even the most confident recent college graduate. Four years of writing lesson plans, researching teaching methods, and participating in student teaching experiences can never fully prepare a new teacher for the challenges encountered upon entering a classroom of his or her own. Perhaps the most important aspect of facilitating a smooth-running learning environment is implementing successful classroom management. There are countless factors to consider when planning how a classroom will be managed.

- How will my classroom be organized?
- How should I set up the rules of the classroom?
- What will my interactions with students be like?
- Which reinforcements should I use?

I ask myself these questions and many more each time I meet a new group of students. As a special education teacher for the past six years,

I have encountered not only students of varying ability, but also students who required a dramatic change in the way I managed my classroom. Strategies that work for students with moderate mental impairments are not always appropriate for students with mild physical disabilities. Likewise, the same type of classroom management may not work even for students with similar abilities. As a beginning teacher, you have some idea of how to manage your own classroom, but trial and error is the only way to discover which methods really work for you.

Organization of the Classroom

One of the first activities a teacher encounters each year is planning the physical layout of the classroom. Although it may not be first on the list of considerations for classroom management, the physical organization of the classroom is very important. For example, if you are using whole-group instruction, then you will likely need to set up the ever-so-common rows of desks with the teacher's location at the front. However, in other situations, such as a resource room, you may have many different activities planned for the same slot of time, so grouped seating may work best. You may even require a mixture of both. In addition, overstimulation in the classroom can create difficulties for students with attention problems. Having too much for students to look at in one area can prove challenging when attempting to keep students on task.

Rules for the Classroom

There are many rules that must be enforced to guarantee a manageable classroom. The hard part is deciding which rules will be implemented, how the rules will be enforced, and how to ensure that the rules are consistently followed. For each new group of students, I am sure to include them in the development of the classroom rules and consequences. Believe it or not, students are often harsher than I am when determining consequences. Whatever the consequences for rule-breaking, you must be consistent with all students when reprimanding. If the students play a part in developing the rules, they will feel like an important part of the classroom and be more likely to follow the rules. Once the rules are decided, they must be posted somewhere that is visible to all students. In addition, wording the classroom rules in a positive manner gets better results than negative wording. For example, instead of stating, "No talking while the teacher is talking," you could say, "Wait your turn to speak." It's amazing how a simple change like wording affects the climate of a classroom. Don't forget that too many rules are overwhelming, so you should try to group as many rules into one category as possible.

Interactions With Students

Your interactions with students have a large impact on how your classroom is managed. In any given school, many different teaching styles are present. Some teachers are very authoritative, while others test the boundaries of a manageable classroom. I live by the philosophy that if I show students respect and listen to their ideas and opinions, then they are more likely to show me respect. This method, however, can be quite frustrating when students test your limits. The rewards, however, outweigh the frustration when you have positive relations with students who are otherwise defiant. Positive interactions are important. I am lucky because my caseload is rather limited, allowing me to show students small gestures, such as giving them birthday cards, so they know someone cares.

Positive Reinforcement

Reinforcements also play an important role in classroom management. Believe it or not, even most high school students enjoy the simple things teachers can do to reinforce positive behavior. Kind words and small tokens are often much appreciated, especially for students who come from imperfect home settings. As trivial as it seems, teenagers also get a kick out of receiving stickers on their papers. A reinforcement I give students on my caseload is a free lunch with me if they pass all their classes each quarter. Once again, this is only manageable for me because I have a small group for which I am responsible.

Summing Up

All in all, everyone develops his or her own classroom management style with time. There are many factors to consider each year when deciding how to facilitate a smoothly running classroom. Whether you intend to be authoritative or to approach your class with a more easygoing attitude, different methods work for different teachers. If one method doesn't work, it is quite simple to try something new. One important thing to remember, however, is that you can always ease up on students as the year progresses, but it is very difficult to go the other way.

▧ 3. Nine Co-Teaching Tips From Two Co-Teaching Gurus

Fonda Akins and Cindy Armitage Dannaker
Springfield, Pennsylvania

Recommended Level: Grades 9–12

Overall Objective: Teachers can use these nine tips to experience success and satisfaction in a co-teaching classroom.

Co-teaching as an art is a continual work in progress. Imagine creating a co-teaching relationship the same way you would a ceramic pot or painting. One begins with a vision in mind, makes the vision a reality using tools, and continues until the final product is satisfying, often changing and revising as if the work is never complete. The tips below can help co-teachers learn to be joint artists, creating their experience together as a unique, moldable work of art.

1. Build a Respectful Relationship

Co-teaching is like a marriage/partnership. Not to scare off potential co-teachers, but effective co-teaching requires the same communication skills as a successful marriage. Forming a relationship of honesty, trust, dedication, and respect is imperative. Although the administration often determines with whom one co-teaches, the best scenario is when co-teachers have input. When preparing to co-teach, teachers should select individuals they respect professionally and get along with personally.

Once the partnership is decided, finding the time to bond, plan in advance, and clarify roles before the students arrive on the first day is imperative. As teaching begins, the importance of talking to one another, not behind each other's backs, cannot be stressed enough. Like a marriage, the pair might need outside help to get through difficult situations, but lots of honest, respectful communication can prevent animosity, distrust, and unprofessional behavior. Keeping egos in check and remembering that the ultimate goal is meeting students' needs helps to keep the relationship on track.

2. Have Co-Planning Time

If teachers are expected to co-teach, co-planning time is necessary. When schedules are organized by the administration, co-teachers' preparation time should be during the same period. If co-teaching is a priority in your school, the administration will schedule inclusion classes first. For example, if a special education teacher co-teaches all English classes, and the entire English department has second period prep, the special education teacher's prep would naturally be second period as well.

Of course, teachers can plan before or after school, but meetings and assisting students often interfere and disrupt this planning time. Without common planning time, true co-teaching is not as likely to occur. If both teachers are going to teach, both teachers need to be onboard with the lesson.

If common planning time is impossible, teachers can still create ways of co-teaching certain lessons through differentiated instruction. For example, if students are creating a class newsletter, and each student has selected an article-type based on comfort level and ability, both teachers can assist all students working independently on the project. On the other hand, if a class has a fair amount of lecture and co-planning time has not occurred, the subject-area teacher will probably do most of the delivery and direct instruction.

Depending on the certification and comfort level of the special education teacher in a subject area, his or her role in different classes may vary. Once again, having the time to plan and discuss allows for more effective teaching and a better co-teaching relationship.

3. Participate in Staff Development

With a focus on mathematics and literacy initiatives and raising state test scores, opportunities for summer or job-embedded staff development for co-teaching may be limited. However, in order for co-teaching relationships to thrive, staff development must occur. If a district doesn't offer co-teaching staff development, there is the possibility of requesting pull-out or compensation time for training with experienced co-teachers.

During staff development, many co-teaching topics should be included: bonding, community building, role clarification, reviewing students' Individualized Education Plans (IEPs), developing strategies to meet students' needs together, discussing content, teaching styles, developing lesson plans, adapting materials, and finding resources and adapted texts.

For co-teaching teams, staff development before school starts can be one of the best ways to get the relationship and classroom climate heading in the right direction. For teachers who don't have the opportunity to meet before school starts, hopefully administrators will realize the importance of co-teaching and will build in staff development time during the first weeks of school in order to work on the previously mentioned topics.

4. Maintain Optimum Class Composition

As a rule of thumb, one-third special education students and two-thirds regular education students is a fair guideline for inclusion classes, aiming for 18 to 21 students, but capping the total at 25 students. Unfortunately, if a school doesn't have enough special education teachers, the number of special education students in inclusion classes will rise above this level, lowering the academic expectations of a regular education class. The possibility of watering down the curriculum is a major concern and can give inclusion classes a bad reputation; inclusion classes are regular education classes with adaptations made for students with special needs. The curriculum remains the same; whether a regular education student is in an inclusion class or not, he or she is entitled to receive the regular curriculum.

When the number of special education students begins to approach the one-half to two-thirds point, the pace of instruction decreases and the regular education students may not experience the full curriculum by the end of the course. This can cause parents of regular education students to oppose having their children in inclusion classes because of the perception that the curriculum was watered-down as a result of the high number of special education students in the class.

On the other hand, if a regular education student needs remediation, his or her parents will sometimes request placement in inclusion classes because of the additional support that is provided. In general, to help maintain the regular education status of the classroom, requests such as this should be declined if the classroom composition already consists of one-third special education and two-thirds regular education. When requests are honored, other parents quickly learn of this option and a regular education class may fall into the category of a lower-level class. Districts need to be mindful about granting such requests (and may consider adopting a policy to address this concern) to maintain the effectiveness of inclusion classes for all students.

5. Define Roles

Before class starts, the roles of the regular education teacher and the special education teacher should be clearly defined. It is the job of the regular education teacher to be the expert in his or her content area. The regular education teacher is responsible for making sure the pace and the rigor of the subject remain the same.

The special education teacher is the expert in making the curriculum accessible to learners with special needs. In the inclusion setting, special education teachers are generally responsible for making adaptations and accommodations to the curriculum. It is essential that the special education teacher not be viewed as a classroom aide. This situation can be avoided by allowing the special educator to deliver instruction to *all* students in the classroom. The regular educator and the special educator should take turns delivering instruction to students. All students can benefit from having two teachers in the classroom. Both the special education and regular education teacher are responsible for implementing IEPs.

6. Develop Adaptations

Adaptations are used in an inclusive classroom setting to help special education students attain academic success in a regular education classroom. The IEP drives the adaptations and accommodations that will meet the student's individual needs, including, but not limited to, the following:

- Provides summaries for each chapter in a novel or textbook.
- Presents students with textbooks and novels on their reading level.
- Differentiates instruction.
- Administers performance-based assessments.
- Focuses on students' strengths and assess to build confidence.
- Gives tests that look similar (i.e., same color paper) so it is not obvious if special education students have different assessments.
- Offers both short answer and essay questions on tests, instead of all essay questions—particularly for struggling writers.
- Asks questions that require straightforward answers, and limit choices for multiple choice-type questions.
- Includes word banks for fill-in-the-blank questions.
- Reads tests aloud and clarify directions for students.
- Orally assesses students in addition to giving them written assessments.
- Reassesses a student to test for skill or content mastery if a student has failed an assessment.
- Allows extended time for assessments, projects, and written assignments. (However, to create responsibility within the learner, provide the ultimate deadline as to when an assignment must be turned in.)
- Supplies graphic organizers for reading and writing assignments.
- Shares samples of well-written essays and projects with students. This will let students know the caliber of work that teachers expect from them.
- Curtails the length of the assignment by one third to one half (including homework and writing assignments).
- Gives students the opportunity to make test corrections and writing assignment revisions for credit.
- Distributes study guides for all major assessments.

- Focuses on teaching the most important aspects of the course; students will better understand important concepts rather than partially understanding many details and facts. Remember, less is more.
- Recognizes that anything that a regular and a special education teacher can do to help any student meet with academic success will benefit all students.

7. Utilize Resources

In order to have a successful classroom that meets various students' learning styles, teachers must utilize all resources inside and outside of the classroom. Paraprofessionals are invaluable in an inclusive classroom. Under the direction of a special education or a regular education teacher, paraprofessionals can assist students one-on-one and in small groups. In addition, placing students in cooperative learning groups with various academic and motivational levels is a useful technique in inclusion classrooms. For example, when a teacher starts a new unit, new chapter, or group project, balancing student groups with varying motivation and ability levels helps high achievers motivate learners with special needs through cooperation.

A successful inclusive school must have a designated area for students in need of extra help with assignments. Students can go to a learning center staffed by a teacher or paraprofessional to take tests, receive academic help (with reading, writing, math, etc.), or to receive assistance in completing projects and homework.

Utilizing students from study halls as learning assistants for special education students both in class and in a learning center is a powerful form of community service. Students can receive credit for school or community service as peer tutors. Quite often, learning-support students feel singled out or embarrassed when a special education teacher tries to help them. Learners with special needs are more receptive when peers assist them with their classwork. And for those considering careers in education, peer tutors are able to explore the area of teaching through their experience.

All-inclusive schools should invest in appropriate and engaging computer programs that will help remediate students' math, reading, and writing skills. Students can and should use these remedial programs during study halls, after school, or during class.

Utilizing adapted literature and textbooks helps learning-support students access the curriculum. Many of the required textbooks used in secondary classrooms are above special education students' reading and comprehension levels. Frustration stemming from an inability to understand can lead to behavior problems, low self-esteem, and low achievement. However, a novel or textbook written on students' reading levels unlocks a world of knowledge and understanding while building confidence in the learners. Providing texts of varying ability levels allows students to select whichever text fits without feeling as if they are being singled out with the easy text.

Utilizing parents as a key support resource benefits both students and teachers. When parents are supportive and aware of learning differences, students feel more confident that they will meet with success.

8. Work Out Co-Teaching Strategies

As mentioned earlier, co-teaching is similar to entering into a new marriage. Before entering into the co-teaching model, co-teachers *must* figure out each other's comfort levels.

Each teacher should decide and agree on which tasks to pursue. Some issues to discuss ahead of time include how to handle housekeeping items such as attendance, checking homework, and managing discipline.

Both teachers must be on the same page to assure successful co-teaching in an inclusive classroom. Some regular education teachers who are new at co-teaching may have problems sharing space and giving up classroom control to another teacher. However, the special education teacher must be viewed as an equal partner in the classroom. It is inappropriate for students to refer to a special educator as an *aide* or a *helper*. Some examples of effective co-teaching include, but are not limited to, the following:

- The class is split into smaller groups and both teachers assist the groups.
- One teacher checks homework, while the other teacher goes over the assignment.
- One teacher explains an activity, while the other teacher walks around the room and checks for understanding prior to undertaking the task.

- Teachers take turns explaining parts of the activity.
- Teachers model an upcoming activity. For example, one teacher reads his or her writing aloud, while the other teacher models a peer response.

9. Communicate

Communication is another crucial element for the success of co-teaching. Co-teachers must honestly communicate their preferences, dislikes, and what they thought went well or wrong with a lesson.

- Plan prior to and debrief after a lesson to create a bond and discover comfort levels.
- Discuss who will teach what, how lessons will be taught, and individual comfort levels to alleviate much of the anxiety around co-teaching relationships.
- Converse about what each teacher needs in the classroom in order for all learners to be successful.
- Help regular education teachers learn how to meet the needs of special education students in regular and inclusion classrooms through conversations with the special education teacher.
- Communicate with students about interests, extracurricular activities, and hobbies to create a student-teacher connection aside from academics. By showing students that both teachers are interested in all students, the stigma of being a special education student is minimized.
- Contact parents about students' progress through e-mail, phone, or conference. This responsibility belongs to both the special education and the regular education teachers. Students, teachers, and parents benefit by being kept informed of progress and occurrences in the lives of students. Many teachers have Web sites parents can log onto to find out what is expected in the classroom.

Co-teaching is similar to creating a work of art, requiring skill, vision, attention to detail, and care. When co-teachers follow the tips presented here, the experience can be a rich, colorful canvas from which they and their students can grow, learn, and experience success.

Differentiated Instruction

Overview, Chapters 4–5

4. **Kristen S. McDaniel**, an economics teacher in Fort Atkinson, Wisconsin, offers key suggestions to help teachers meet the needs of all learners in a secondary classroom.

5. **Christine Roland**, a science teacher in Edgewood, Maryland, prevents reviewing and re-teaching from turning into monotonous exercises with a differentiated approach that changes plain reviews into delectable Review Buffets.

4. Every Student Has a Story: Students With Special Needs and English Language Learners in the Secondary Classroom

Kristen S. McDaniel
Fort Atkinson, Wisconsin

Recommended Level: Grades 9–12

Overall Objective: Teachers can use these guidelines to welcome students with special needs and English language learners into the general classroom community with confidence.

Every student in your classroom has a story that is vital to the success of the class. Oprah Winfrey says that everyone has a story, but

I will take that one step further. Every student's story is important, and understanding that story not only assists the individual student with his or her education, it also teaches others in your class about diversity and acceptance. Federal law guarantees access to education to those students who might be different from those in the mainstream classroom, but a teacher must take those differences and use them to teach all the students in the class valuable lessons.

Students with special needs, whether they have an IEP or a plan under Section 504, as well as students whose primary language is not English, need four things from teachers:

- The knowledge that someone cares
- A little more assistance in comprehending course concepts and skills
- A safe environment
- A lack of isolation

A learning situation that reflects these conditions can benefit all students, but it is critical for students with special needs.

For a subject-area teacher in a secondary school, this can be challenging. Seeing 120 or more students in a day can make it very difficult to differentiate instruction for students who may need language instruction or reading and comprehension assistance. In addition, many subject area classroom teachers have not had a lot of training regarding the needs of students with IEPs, 504 plans, or those still learning English. This combination can leave classroom teachers confused and frustrated about how to make sure students with special needs receive the education they deserve.

Subject-area teachers, however, can make their classroom a safe place for all students. Building relationships with students and special-needs staff, ensuring that classroom rules make the room a place where all students give and receive respect, and offering accommodations to students will allow the students in the classroom to metaphorically tell their story. These stories blend together to create the distinct rapport that a teacher has with each classroom, and they allow learning to happen.

Teachers' relationships with their students are the most important part of the equation. Perfectly differentiated lesson plans will fall flat if the teacher does not have rapport with his or her students. Building a relationship of trust should always be a teacher's first priority at the beginning of a term. This doesn't have to be an enormous deal that takes a large amount of time; in fact, doing small things over the course of many days will make the rapport stronger. Greeting all students at the door and asking them how their weekend was or how their day is going is a great way to start. If you have English language learners in your classroom, learn how to greet them in their native language. I often find out how to do so on my own and surprise them one day, just to see their eyes light up. Usually, they will be very pleased that a teacher took the time to learn even that little bit of their language. Joking with students and being willing to laugh at yourself is also a good way to build rapport in your classroom. Taking the time to talk to students as individuals makes them realize that their teachers care about their success in the classroom. I am not going to suggest you call all your students' homes four times a week, but I will say that a three minute conversation one day about what they find important can create a bond. A smile and a question about that conversation a week later can help cement that bond.

Building relationships with staff that have more training with students with special needs will assist in determining what will best fit a student's needs. Special education teachers, the 504 coordinator, reading and literacy specialists, caseworkers, and English language learner (ELL)/ESL teachers have background information on and experience with what will work with different students. Their toolbox is bigger, and they are usually delighted to help subject-area teachers who are looking for ways to reach a student. In most cases, they know the student already and have either worked with him or her previously, know previous caseworkers and teachers who have worked with that individual student, or just have a good idea of research-based information on best practices with students who have similar learning disabilities.

Offering a safe place for all students is vitally important for every teacher, with every class they have. No student should be subject to ridicule, no matter what is going on. This is especially true for students with special needs, only because they probably face it more than others. Don't allow students to make fun of others, and don't allow gossip in the classroom. Punishment for teasing should be immediate, and a teacher should never, ever contribute to personal teasing of a student. Never single out a student with special needs; all teenagers crave acceptance from peers and do not want others to realize that they might be different, even if they have gone to school together for many years. I have experienced situations in which a student with special needs entered a class late on the first day and heard other students groan or sigh. Making them realize that such actions are totally unacceptable is vitally important for the safety and comfort level of the students with special needs.

Students who are struggling with English as the primary source of lessons should never be isolated. Instead, bring them into groups, invite them to work with others, and pair them with a buddy. Every student needs to feel that they have something worthwhile to offer and that they are free to give that information in your classroom without having to fear ridicule or reprisal.

I purposely selected accommodating and modifying curriculum as the final suggestion for making sure students with special needs find success in your classroom. Most IEPs and 504 plans will offer accommodations, and most ELL/ESL teachers will have ideas on how to adapt curriculum to meet the needs of students. Read the IEPs and 504 plans carefully, and if you have any questions, contact the student's caseworker. Never point out to individual students in front of the class what their accommodations might be, and don't make a big deal about it. The policy where I work allows students who might normally leave the room to take a test to start it in class, but to write at the top of the test "Please give to Mrs. X.," so while I am going through their tests, I know that the student felt they needed more time, or needed something read to them, and I was to put their test in Mrs. X's mailbox so the student could finish the assessment. This is a great policy to allow students to stay with their peers, to not face the staring or ridicule of leaving the class to go to the "SPED" room to take a test, yet still have their needs met.

For students still learning English, taking a few minutes to go online to a free translation site such as http://www.freetranslator.com offers a chance to put any assignment or assessment into the child's first language. Although not a perfect translation, it is enough for many students to get the general idea and shows that you are taking the time to help them. It creates a bond, and it demonstrates that you care. This, perhaps, is even more important than the academic concepts they might learn in your class.

Both students with special needs and English language learners should be graded against their own progress, rather than being compared to the class as a whole. In a perfect world, each student would be assessed on their own individual progress, but of course, we do not have the time or resources to do such a thing. For these students, however, it is vital that they are assessed on their own knowledge. One great way to assess progress in any course is through a portfolio. Students keep track of the journey on their own, and they choose the assignments, projects, and other assessments that they feel show their learning the best. This works especially well with students still learning English because a teacher can tailor the portfolio to the need of the child. Language can be a barrier to learning, but that barrier can be torn down by the relationships that teachers can build with their students.

The stories that students tell are very important. It's not only good for students to understand and live with diversity—it's vital. The words that students with special needs bring to the story of your classroom are the adjectives and adverbs, the voice and the flow. Without that variety, classes become dull and boring, like a book without a good plotline. Regular education students in your classroom learn from students with special needs, just as those students learn from "normal" ones. In a globalized society, one of the most important skills that students learn is to get along with people of different backgrounds; having students that might be different from others in the classroom is the first key in learning this valuable skill.

℞ 5. Buffet-Style Teaching: Reviewing and Re-Teaching

Christine Roland
Edgewood, Maryland

Recommended Level: Grade 10

Overall Objective: Students will reflect on what areas they need to review and will choose and complete an appropriate activity to review and relearn material that was previously taught.

Standards Met (National Science Education): The program of study in science for all students should be developmentally appropriate, interesting, and relevant to students' lives; should emphasize student understanding through inquiry; and should be connected with other school subjects. Science content must be embedded in a variety of curriculum patterns that are developmentally appropriate, interesting, and relevant to students' lives.[1]

Materials Needed:

- Student handouts
- Activity directions (laminated)
- Small baskets
- Scissors
- Glue
- Miscellaneous craft supplies
- 2 × 3 foot blackboards and chalk

To prevent reviewing and re-teaching from turning into monotonous exercises, a differentiated approach becomes manageable when plain reviews are changed into delicious all-you-can-eat Review Buffets. The following is an example of how I introduce a buffet style review in my classroom:

Today we are going to feast on a scientific buffet! In this buffet, you will find a variety of deliciously short activities and assignments, designed to review everything you need to know and might have forgotten about this unit. For those of you who are not so sure you have mastered a topic or concept, stick with the plainer, more basic items for that particular area of the buffet. Those of you who are feeling a little more adventurous, though, go ahead and get a serving of something spicier to challenge your mental taste buds and discover nuances you may not have considered before. And finally, for those of you who have gotten your fill over the last couple of weeks, and feel you have mastered this topic, try one of the sumptuous desserts and discover a whole new serving of this material.

A Review Buffet is designed to give students choices, not only to accommodate their different learning styles and individual levels of understanding. It is meant to offer something for everyone to make sure all students have an opportunity to relearn and deepen their knowledge.

Review and *differentiation* are terms that rarely coincide. Reviews often are teacher-centered explanations, study guides, or a class game of *Jeopardy*. Differentiation at the end of a unit seems to fall by the wayside and can easily become forgotten amidst time constraints and test pressures. Yet this is precisely the time where differentiation becomes essential for student success. At the end of the unit, differences in student understanding vary greatly. While some may indeed have mastered the material, more than likely there are still those who have gaps in their knowledge or simply struggle with the topic. When it comes to re-teaching and reviewing, one size definitely does not fit all, and the idea of differentiation is central to success.

Buffet Design and Planning

Any caterer knows that there are three basic ingredients that make a buffet successful: variety, quality, and balance. Meat and potatoes alone are not going to do it. A "vegetarian option" (providing additional support in the form of calculators, cheat sheets, etc.) for students who might struggle in math is essential in order to get meaningful student data analysis in a science class. Students who don't have the basics need to limit the hard-to-digest material and consume a "low-fat version" first in order to get the extra time to grasp the major concepts. However, a fancy dessert for those who are done with their main course and are still hungry for more is a must in order to challenge and engage those students.

But perhaps the most important aspect of any buffet is simply that it has to be attractive! The items on the buffet need to be presented in an irresistible and appetizing fashion but must also be delicious and nutritious as well as carefully prepared. This may sound like a lot of work, and it is the first few times, but the result and increase in student success will make this practice a regular one. The key is to find good recipes without having to start from scratch every single time and to add to the cookbook throughout the year.

How to Build a Buffet

1. Choose the Critical Thinking Level of Buffet Items

Turning a simple idea into something more engaging, especially a short buffet item, is actually not as time-consuming as it may first appear. The initial step is to choose the critical thinking level for the exercise using Bloom's (1956) taxonomic levels of critical thinking:

1. *Knowledge*—Define, describe, identify, label, match, outline

2. *Comprehension*—Compare/contrast, characterize, summarize, generalize, categorize

3. *Application*—Apply, model, classify, draw, change, construct, perform, present

4. *Analysis*—Analyze, categorize, correlate, diagram, differentiate, explain, construct

5. *Synthesis*—Combine, connect, create, design, develop, hypothesize, judge, organize

6. *Evaluate*—Assess, defend, critique, debate, recommend, judge

Then combine Bloom's levels with some basic activity ideas. This allows you to quickly choose assignments for cognitively different levels. For example, when creating a buffet for science, the "plain option" is pulled from Levels 1 and 2 of Bloom's taxonomy. For "spicy" items, I choose verbs from Levels 3 and 4, and I reserve "sweet items" generally for Levels 5 and 6.

2. Find Activities

Teachers tend to be packrats, and most of us have folders filled with little bits and pieces of instructional strategies. Some are used on a regular basis, while others are simply stored away and forgotten. However, these short and quick little tidbits provide a wealth of ideas on how to package content for a buffet. Graphic organizers can be reinvented into sorting and categorizing items, while vocabulary strategies and games can provide the basis for some spicy morsels on the buffet. Story writing and poetry (yes, even in science) could lend a touch of sweetness and diversify the buffet to everyone's taste.

Another place to find ideas is in textbooks and the accompanying teacher materials. Many textbooks have mini labs and short activities that often provide an excellent starting point for a buffet item. Many activities within a chapter are meant to provide short vignettes and can easily be adapted to a buffet item.

The Internet, though, is the place where lessons and ideas are most abundant. One drawback that can occur is that the search for a single buffet item can turn into hours of Web surfing. It is more efficient to have a full but basic menu for the buffet in mind in order to search for multiple items simultaneously. I don't go online until I have already established the overall composition of my buffet and I am simply looking for a few ideas to add flavoring to what I already have.

3. Make It Yummy

The novelty appeal and "yummy factor" for all buffet items comes through the delivery. Instead of using paper and pen, provide 2×3 foot blackboards and chalk and invite students to discuss and record solutions and change them as they evolve. Sorting, categorizing, and organizing become much more appealing when cards with pictures, diagrams, and objects are used instead of filling in boxes on a graphic organizer. Simple modifications like cutting and pasting quickly increase the level of engagement and help students to make new connections. All of these things promote collaborative learning and help raise the appeal of the buffet. Both plain and spicy items might include games like Pictionary, Memory, and hangman, while dessert includes activities that are more independent and self-guided extensions.

Vegetarian and low-fat options provide additional support for students working on buffet items. Calculators, labeled diagrams, and vocabulary explanations can all provide the extra utensils needed for students to succeed and learn the material presented.

4. Build a Strong Recipe Collection

Review Buffets grow over time. They become more elaborate and refined each year. Just like cooks who collect recipes when they happen to come across them, the search and hunt for buffet items becomes second nature, and buffets can evolve alongside regular lesson planning.

Characteristics of a Good Buffet Item

- Differentiated: An activity should reflect different learning styles and critical thinking levels to appeal to many palates.
- Linked to objectives: The item is directly linked to an objective from a previous lesson and takes into account the previous meal and the next one. Don't serve breakfast at night.
- Concise and clear: Students need instructions that enable them to do the activity independently.
- Appropriate in length: Depending on class length, a buffet item should be doable in 15 to 30 minutes.
- Novel and appetizing: While the content is not new, the activity has to be different from activities done in previous classes.

Example: Genetics Review Buffet

Genetics is a major unit in my biology classes. At the end of this unit, I give my students two 90-minute periods to work through the Genetics Review Buffet (see Figure 5.1). This buffet consists of 12 different activities, including four plain, six spicy, and two sweet items. Each student is expected to work through four to six activities, with at least one from each category, during the time provided. The content is broken up into the following categories:

- Mendelian genetics and Punnett squares (six activities)
- Karyotypes and chromosomal disorders (three activities)
- Pedigrees and sex-linked traits (three activities)

Figure 5.1   Example: Genetics Review Buffet (Mendelian Genetics and Punnett Squares)

1. Knowledge	2. Comprehension	3. Application
Plain: Critter Cards	**Plain: Gene Chips**	**Spicy: Ugly Bugs**
Identify genotoype and phenotype ratios. Practice Punnett square problems. Students are given Critter Cards showing the phenotypes of different traits. They use the cards to practice Punnett squares.	*Categorize and discuss* genotypes and phenotypes. For students who need basic instruction combined with a hands-on and collaborative approach. Counting chips are used to represent single chromosomes. Each side of the chip has a letter showing the specific allele with two alleles adding up to a genotype.	*Construct* a simple organism (ugly bug) with four traits and *model* their inheritance through three generations.
4. Analysis	5. Synthesis	6. Evaluation
Spicy: Mendelian Easter Eggs	**Sweet: Corn Snake Genetics**	**Sweet: Genetic Counseling**
Analyze the phenotype ratios of offspring to determine parental genotypes. Easter eggs containing beads represent a family (½ egg = Mom, ½ egg = Dad, beads represent offspring) Color is used as the genetic trait examined and the ratios of the offspring are used to determine genotypes of the parents.	*Hypothesize* about the mode of inheritance of corn snakes based on pictures. Students study picture cards of corn snakes and provide an explanation about the mode of inheritance that results in the observed phenotypes.	*Critique* the report from a genetic counselor to a couple expecting a child with sickle cell.

All buffet items are on a buffet table in the classroom. Each item is completely self-contained and packaged in a basket. Baskets are labeled according to content and difficulty level (plain, spicy, and sweet) and include laminated directions, student hand-outs, and all materials needed (scissors, glue, craft supplies, etc.) to complete the activity. Students take the entire basket back to their tables and work at their own pace. I usually offer most items in duplicates, so more than one student or group can work on it at the same time.

Note

1. Reprinted with permission from *National Science Education Standards,* 1996, by the National Academy of Sciences, courtesy of the National Academies Press, Washington, D.C.

Reference

Bloom, B. S. (1956). *Taxonomy of educational objectives, handbook I: The cognitive domain.* New York: David McKay.

Using Technology in the Classroom

⧉ 6. Using Technology Doesn't Have to Be Expensive

Cindy Couchman
Buhler, Kansas

Recommended Level: Grades 9–12

Overall Objective: Teachers can encourage students' learning through the creative and inexpensive use of technology across all subjects.

When using technology in the classroom, many of us immediately envision the use of a laptop or a complicated computer program. Since

29

many schools across the nation do not have one-to-one laptop initiatives in their districts, we have to rethink our definition of technology. When I first started teaching, technology meant *computer*. The 21st-century learners we have in class now have a different definition and experience with technology. Here are some ideas on how to use technology (cheaply) and spice up your projects and presentations!

To organize student assignments and resources, instructors can create a class wiki and a portaportal. When studying different historical sites or cultures, use Google Earth to take a virtual tour of any location in the world! In math, using flip cameras to record students working a problem more than one way provides students with excellent practice in learning to communicate mathematically.

Make the traditional report on an important person in history more engaging for students by having them research someone and create movies that include photos, video clips, and music using iDVD.

Perhaps you are a business instructor and looking for a new project. Have students use Comic Life, Keynote, or PowerPoint to create brochures or radio infomercials to share what they have learned. Students could create business cards for themselves or others using this dynamic software.

Using Facebook, our students' preferred social networking resource, communication arts teachers can create "Groups" and invite students to be "Friends." The instructor can then set up a discussion and post a series of questions that students are required to respond to. Students can interact with each other, sharing ideas, reflections, and questions about stories they are reading. This allows the instructor to guide and monitor these virtual learning experiences.

Use technology to help class members get acquainted with each other at the beginning of the year by having students create a personal video biography or having them type a biography and use Wordle collages to give a visual summary of themselves.

In foreign language classes, a blog can be used to have students write responses to a topic posted by an instructor in the language they are studying. Students can use their cell phones to create podcasts reading poetry in that language, and can then listen to each other and critique the reading. How about using ePals to connect with students from another country to form a global learning environment? Posting YouTube videos using a flip camera is a great way to reinforce grammar as students present subjunctive tense.

Using technology doesn't have to be expensive or time consuming, and it doesn't have to detract from the curriculum. Technology should enhance your curriculum and instruction and engage our 21st-century learners!

⧉ 7. Using Computer-Assisted Instruction in High School Mathematics Classes

Suzanne Blair
Gardner, Kansas

Recommended Level: Grades 10–12 (Algebra I)

Overall Objective: Students will overcome previous difficulties with math and progress successfully through Algebra I with computer-assisted instruction.

As technology advances, we as teachers need to consider alternatives to whole-group instruction. For classes above or below grade level, computer-assisted instruction may be an option. Last year, Gardner Edgerton High School decided to try using computer-assisted instruction for Algebra I classes with students in Grades 10 through 12. Throughout the process of using software to teach an Algebra I class for the first time, advantages and challenges were discovered.

The high school chose a Web-based program, ALEKS, because of its artificial intelligence in assessing students. This program offered a pretest in which each question was selected based on the students' answers to previous questions. The program assessed many prerequisites required for learning Algebra I and eventually re-taught the prerequisites to individual students if needed. The advantages of the program included that lessons were reassigned when needed and that students were able to progress quickly through the program if they did well on tests. Other advantages included the online training, the ease of creating student accounts, and the individualized learning plans.

During the summer before implementation, teachers were trained using online materials provided by the company, including video lessons. The training was invaluable and enabled the teachers involved to become comfortable with the program before the school year began.

During the first two weeks of the school year, teachers used traditional classroom methods of instruction to review students' math skills related to solving equations, graphing linear equations, probability, and statistics. The students then began working with the software the third week of school. The process of having students create user IDs and passwords went smoothly due to the summer training. Once students were logged into the program, a tutorial was given showing students how to input answers and how to graph lines in the program. This particular program does not ask any multiple-choice questions. All answers are inputted in a way that is similar to writing answers using pencil and paper.

Students were continually assessed throughout the use of the program. Assessments can be assigned by the teacher at any time. In addition, the program assigned an assessment after a certain number of lessons had been completed. After an assessment was completed, the program for each student was adjusted. If the student correctly answered questions over lessons that the student had not completed, the program gave them credit for those lessons. On the other hand, if the student missed questions over material that the student had worked on, the program made them rework those lessons.

Once students finished the pretest in the program, individualized learning plans were established. Many students seemed uneasy at first with their individualized programs. After becoming familiar with the program and working in it for a week or so, the students began progressing through lessons using the tutoring within the program and tutoring from the teachers. Students also began helping each other with lessons and teaching each other. Students received immediate feedback in the program, so if someone was not completing problems correctly, the difficulties were quickly exposed.

Some areas of concern were found when implementing this program in our school for the first time. The teachers struggled with staffing, students who did not make progress compared to peers, and grading. These difficulties have been easy to fix due to the flexibility of paraprofessionals that work with our special education students and changes in our philosophy of assigning grades.

Individual tutoring is needed for students within a classroom. Teachers must seek assistance from paraprofessionals and others available in the community for tutoring. Older, more advanced students may need community service hours, and these students may be willing to help tutor. Schools implementing computer-assisted instruction need to keep class sizes to a minimum to assure students will have proper assistance. Small-group tutoring may be used if software allows you to list the students who are working on particular concepts.

The program we used made it easy to identify students that needed further assistance from the professional staff in the building. The tracking systems available showed students who were not making progress in relation to their peers. When a student did not make progress, we provided tutoring within the classroom and during a separate math lab session outside of class. When students were not making progress with tutoring in place, the parents and counselor of the student were contacted. Students were referred to our problem-solving intervention team.

Grading students on a traditional scale did not seem fair to students. With the software our school had chosen, the decision was made to grade students using the students' number of lessons completed, total hours logged in the program, and homework scores on traditional assignments related to reviewing concepts on the Kansas Mathematics Assessment. We had to look at many ideas for grading that were untraditional, such as not including test grades because the tests became harder when students did well on initial questions.

Our grading system is as follows:

Percentage of Objectives Mastered (30%)

Hours Logged (30%)

District Quarterly Test Scores (10%)

Homework/Classwork/Quizzes (30%)

The students had goals for hours and lessons logged in the program for each end of a grading period, including progress reports. The goals for the percentage of lessons completed were the following:

Progress report Quarter 1	12.5%
Quarter 1	25%
Progress report Quarter 2	37.5%
Quarter 2	50%
Progress report Quarter 3	62.5%
Quarter 3	75%
Progress report Quarter 4	87.5%
Quarter 4	100%

The grades were determined by dividing the percentage completed by the percentage expected. In addition, the hours logged in the program were determined based on the number of classes during each grading period. The hours needed were as follows for the year:

Progress report Quarter 1	7.5 hours by September 10
Quarter 1	14.5 hours by October 7
Progress report Quarter 2	25.5 hours by November 11
Quarter 2	33.5 hours by December 15
Progress report Quarter 3	45.5 hours by February 6
Quarter 3	54.5 hours by March 10
Progress report Quarter 4	64.5 hours by April 14
Quarter 4	73.5 hours by May 19

Percentage of hours logged out of hours expected was converted to a 100 point grade in the grade book before progress reports and grade cards. Students who were absent, or were not working during class when they were supposed to be, fell short in hours. Absent students were asked to work on the program during math lab or time outside of the school day at home or at school.

Students who began the year late presented a challenge. After the pretest in the program, those students were given individual goals to complete the program. The students were still asked to complete the entire program by the end of the year. Any student that did not complete the entire program—all 238 lessons—was not given credit—except for special circumstances where students had different goals written in an individualized education plan.

Computer-assisted software may be taking the place of traditional instruction in some mathematics classes. These programs have some clear advantages and disadvantages. Programs that are tailored to the needs of individual students and reassess students on a regular basis are beneficial to mathematics programs. Difficulties with starting computer-aided instruction include grading and staffing. When students need individual attention, it is necessary to have more than one professional in the classroom to meet these needs.

Overall, the program has been a success. With the adjustments we have made throughout the year, many students who were previously unsuccessful at math have been able to reach some difficult goals within the programs. The students have responded by helping each other and working consistently. Hopefully, computer-assisted instruction will remain a part of our mathematics curriculum for many years to come.

▧ 8. Video Analysis Unlocks the Physics World

Timothy Couillard and Robert Benway
Midlothian, Virginia

Recommended Level: Grades 11–12

Overall Objective: Students will learn to film a short video clip for scientific analysis, import that video clip into software for analysis, analyze short video clips and create a graph of two-dimensional motion, and mathematically model data to describe motion in two dimensions.

Standards Met (Virginia): Physics: The student will plan and conduct investigations in which the components of a system are defined; instruments are selected and used to extend observations and measurements of mass, volume, temperature, heat exchange, energy transformations, motion, fields, and electric charge; information is recorded and presented in an organized format; metric units are used in all measurements and calculations; the limitations of the experimental apparatus and design are recognized; and appropriate technology, including computers, graphing calculators, and probeware, is used for gathering and analyzing data and communicating results. The student will investigate and understand how to analyze and interpret data. Key concepts include a description of a physical problem is translated into a mathematical statement in order to find a solution; relationships between physical quantities are determined using the shape of a curve passing through experimentally obtained data; the slope of a linear relationship is calculated and includes appropriate units. The student will investigate and understand how to demonstrate scientific reasoning and logic. Key concepts include analysis of scientific sources to develop and refine research hypotheses; analysis of how science explains and predicts relationships; evaluation of evidence for scientific theories; and construction and defense of a scientific viewpoint (the nature of science). The student will investigate and understand the interrelationships among mass, distance, force, and time through mathematical and experimental processes. Key concepts include linear motion and projectile motion.

Materials Needed:

- Meter stick (or measuring tape)
- Digital camera (with video capability) or a video camera
- USB or Firewire cable, depending on the type of camera and computer
- Tripod
- Desktop or laptop computer
- One of the following software programs:
  - LoggerPro by Vernier Software and Technology (http://www.vernier.com/soft/lp.html)
  - Tracker (http://www.cabrillo.edu/~dbrown/tracker/)
  - VideoPoint (http://www.lsw.com/videopoint/)

In this project, students investigate the mathematical models that describe two-dimensional motion. They do this by capturing two-dimensional motion of their own creation and downloading it into one of several available motion-analysis programs. After calibrating the scale of the video, they do a dot analysis that plots the motion in the clip as an object translates across the field of view. Once the dot analysis is complete, students have a data set that they then attempt to model mathematically using a best-fit curve. This can be done manually with students testing different coefficients in the equations or the process can be automated to give the students the optimal solution. The following are instructions to students to guide them through this lesson.

Activity 1: Capturing Your Video

1. Brainstorm a motion experiment to film. Keep in mind that you want a motion that is clearly visible to the camera.

2. Film the motion. Consult the directions for your video or digital camera for assistance. Use a whiteboard or a piece of paper to label the clip at the beginning of the video. Give it a title, the name of the student group, and the number of the trial if you are doing multiple takes (see Figure 8.1). This will help you download the right clip to the right lab group for analysis.

3. Do several takes so that you can choose the best clip to analyze.

4. Consider these tips:

   ■ Choose either a dark object against a bright background or a bright object against a dark background. For example, hang a dark colored sheet behind the motion for best contrast.
   ■ Place a meter stick in the frame so that it is clearly visible. Alternatively, measure the length of something else that is clearly visible in the shot. For example, if you are using a ball, know its diameter.
   ■ Make sure that your video camera or digital camera is in a fixed position. A tripod is highly recommended.

■ Make sure that your video camera or digital camera is set up so that the lens is perpendicular to the plane of motion. This will lead to more accurate results.

Figure 8.1

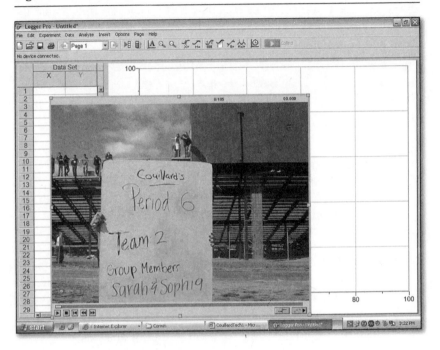

Activity 2: Downloading Your Video Clip
and Importing It Into the Analysis Software

1. Plug the camera in to the computer using a USB or firewire cable.

2. Follow the instructions specific to your type of camera, computer, and software for downloading to the computer.

3. Create a folder for the video clips and name the files using identifiable information, such as lab group name, class period, take number, and so on.

4. Open up the video analysis software of your choice.

5. Import or insert the video clip into the program. See the software for specific instructions.

Activity 3: Analyzing Your Video

Your video should now be imported into your software and ready for analysis.

1. First set the scale of distance in the frame. This is usually done by drawing a line along a known distance (in this case, the meter stick located to the immediate left of the white bucket being dropped; see Figure 8.2).

2. Next, using the marker tool, pick a point on the moving object and mark the position in each frame (see Figure 8.3).

3. Using the graphing feature of the software, you can format a graph of vertical or horizontal position data (see Figure 8.4).

4. Using the mathematical modeling features of the software, create a best-fit line and identify the coefficients (see Figure 8.5). Students can enter the coefficients manually or try a variety of different equations automatically (see Figure 8.6).

Figure 8.2

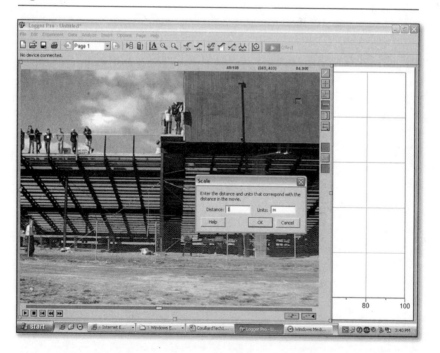

Figure 8.3

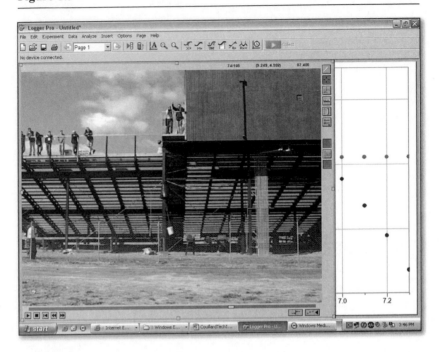

Figure 8.4

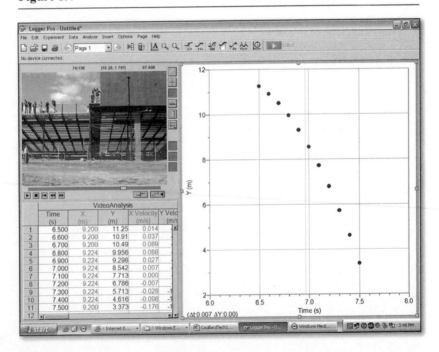

Figure 8.5

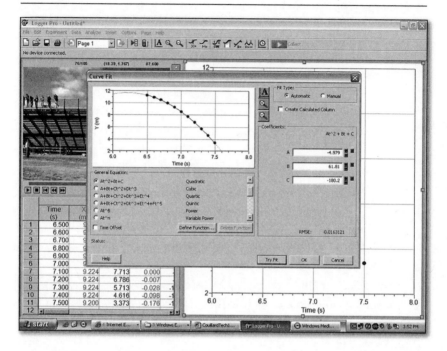

Figure 8.6

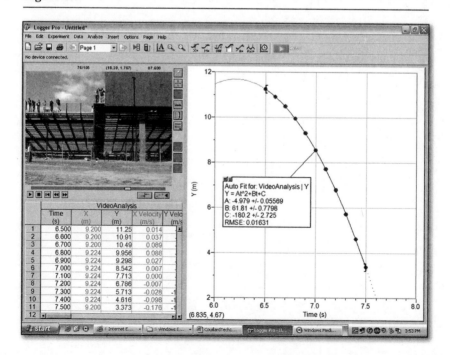

Helpful Tips

- This lesson is designed for all levels of physics, from a qualitative conceptual discussion to advanced manual modeling by AP students.
- What makes this lesson so powerful is that students are able to capture motion of their own design and creation and, in doing so, discover the connection between those authentic physical situations and the mathematics that physicists use to describe them. These new technologies enable the students' realization that physics is rooted in the describing and modeling of the real experiences they find all around themselves every day.
- In addition to the motion that the students capture themselves, there is a wealth of video clips archived by various physics institutions around the world. A few such resources follow:

Brown, D. (2009, August 12). *Video modeling: Combining dynamic model simulations with traditional video analysis.* http://www.compadre.org/OSP/document/ServeFile.cfm?ID=7844&DocID=633

Doane College Physics Department Physics Video Library. http://physics.doane.edu/physicsvideolibrary/default.html

Laws, P., & Pfister, H. (1998). Using digital video analysis in introductory mechanics projects. *The Physics Teacher, 36,* 282–287. physics.dickinson.edu/~dept_web/activities/papers/Video Analysis.pdf

The LivePhoto Physics Project. http://livephoto.rit.edu/

North Carolina School of Science and Mathematics. http://courses.ncssm.edu/physics/video.htm

Tracker-Free Video Analysis and Modeling Tool for Physics Education. http://www.cabrillo.edu/~dbrown/tracker/

Video Analysis Investigations for Physics and Mathematics. http://www3.science.tamu.edu/cmse/videoanalysis/

Wake Forest Department of Physics. http://www.wfu.edu/physics/demolabs/demos/avimov/

Wyrembeck, E. P. (2005, April). *Video analysis with a web camera.* http://www.phys.uwosh.edu/lattery/mps/docs/video_web.pdf

PART II

Teaching Science and Math

Teaching Science

Overview, Chapters 9–15

9. **Christina M. Charles,** a biology teacher in Deerfield, Wisconsin, guides her students in a project to compare and contrast different fertilizing options. The students record and analyze the productivity of fertilizers, draw conclusions from data, and connect the experiment to current events.

10. **Shane McKay,** an anatomy and physiology teacher in San Antonio, Texas, teaches the basic bodily functions by having students develop a narrative, first-person account of a normal homeostatic response from a cellular-level vantage point. Then the students record their narratives as a podcast to post on the Web.

11. **J-Petrina McCarty-Puhl,** a forensic science teacher in Reno, Nevada, engages students by making a connection to the examination of soil at a crime scene. In this project, they investigate the various properties of soil by determining density; percent composition of sand, silt, and clay; and color comparison.

12. **Chris Dodds,** an industrial technology teacher in Greenfield, Ohio, introduces his students to the importance of clean water in a four-day unit on water purification, including a hands-on experiment.

13. **Ann Shioji,** a science teacher in San Jose, California, gives students manipulatives to use in building an atom with protons, neutrons, and electrons. Presented in a bingo game format, this activity motivates students not reached with more traditional teaching methods.

14. **Jeffery R. Wehr,** a science teacher in Odessa, Washington, has students create a working model/expression that conveys the quantum numbers describing the electron configuration of a specific element. The students can choose any academic discipline, such as business, fine arts, humanities, industrial arts, mathematics, or social sciences, in which to work in creating their model.

15. **Jeffery R. Wehr** presents another lesson in which students cooperatively traverse an unknown environment by operating a moving remote-sensing device to collect audio and video data indicating the environment's geophysical properties.

℞ 9. Fertilizers: Testing Different Options

Christina M. Charles
Deerfield, Wisconsin

Recommended Level: Grades 10–12

Overall Objective: Students will generate an experiment to test and compare conventional and alternative fertilizers (worm compost).

Standards Met (Wisconsin): During investigations, choose the best data-collection procedures and materials available, use them competently, and calculate the degree of precision of the resulting data; Evaluate articles and reports in the popular press, in scientific journals, on television, and on the Internet, using criteria related to accuracy, degree of error, sampling, treatment of data, and other standards of experimental design; Analyze the costs, benefits, or problems resulting from a scientific or technological innovation, including implications for the individual and the community; Advocate a solution or combination of solutions to a problem in science or technology; Investigate how current plans or proposals concerning resource management, scientific knowledge, or technological development will have an impact on the environment, ecology, and quality of life in a community or region.

Materials Needed:

All materials listed are for six tables of four students each.

- Planters
- Potting soil
- Commercially available fertilizer
- Vermicompost
- Flowers
- Rulers
- Composition books
- Graphic organizer— Venn diagram

- NPR broadcast: "Scotts Sues Startup Over Worm-Dropping Claims" (story ID: 14149823)
- Reference Web sites for MiracleGro and worm compost
- *Worms Eat My Garbage,* by Mary Appelhof
- Clip of *Dirty Jobs*: "Worm Rancher"

In the fertilizer industry, big-name companies tend to rule the market. While they deliver results for gardeners, alternative methods are often overlooked and underemphasized. As future consumers, students should be educated about all methods of gardening, rather than only the most recognizable and dominant ones. In this unit, students compare a traditional fertilizer from a big-name company with fertilizer from the school-based worm composting project, and they do relevant background research on the similarities and differences between the products. This unit helps to inform students about possible choices for the care of plants at school and at home. In addition, it provides them with the opportunity to make an educated choice about which products they choose to buy for their gardening needs, and it makes them more aware of the gardening (and farming) practices of the providers from which they buy their food and flowers. The following schedule for the project is based on a block system.

Day 1

- Introduce problem: Not many fertilizer options at the store.
- Discuss the possibility of other options—as consumers, options are good.
- Introduce the vermicompost option, and play the National Public Radio (NPR) broadcast of the Scotts story.

- Ask students to write in their journals about their thoughts on the issue. Guiding questions include the following:
  - Why do you think that Scotts is suing TerraCycle?
  - Do you think that it is a good idea to make product superiority claims?
  - Do you think that the lawsuit is truly about product superiority claims?
  - As a consumer, what do you think about having choices?
- Make the issue a testable question—set up an experiment (to be recorded in composition books).
- With student input, design an experiment to test TerraCycle claims.
- Have students combine soil and fertilizer treatment together in planters and add plants.
- Guide students in the creation of a data table to record plant growth and observations over the next month.

Day 2: Student Activities

- Measure growth as determined by the experimental design; record qualitative observations in the data table.
- Analyze the ingredients in commercial and vermicompost fertilizers.
- Research ingredients of interest for possible health and environmental side effects.

Day 3: Student Activities

- Measure the growth of plants and record observations in the data table.
- In two groups, use *Worms Eat My Garbage* as a resource to learn about vermicomposting.
- Research how conventional fertilizer works.
- Compare and contrast conventional and vermicompost fertilizer with a Venn diagram.

Day 4: Student Activities

- Measure the growth of plants and record observations in the data table.

- Watch a clip from *Dirty Jobs*: "Worm Rancher."
- Compare with school's vermicomposting system.
- Discuss ideas for increasing the scale of the school's vermicomposting system.

Days 5–27: Student Activities

- Continue to take measurements and to record data and observations in the data table.

Day 28: Student Activities

- Take final measurement and record data and observations in the data table.
- Analyze data and draw conclusions.
- Use the experiment as a reference for future school gardening procedure.
- Write a final journal entry that includes the following:
  - An analysis of the results of the study
  - Ideas for implications about how we should fertilize the soil in our school garden
  - Final thoughts about the Scotts case, as well as *informed* consumer choice
  - Discuss ideas, feelings, and so on in class

Evaluation of the Project and Assessment of Student Work

This project can be evaluated on the basis of

- The quality of student-generated experimental procedure and recorded data
- Class discussion—participation, insight
- Student assessment results

The rubrics that follow represent one option for grading journal entries. Different weights are assigned to different journal criteria to create a hierarchy of emphasis: Scientific concepts are given the most weight, followed by reflective practices, and then writing quality. With a rubric, students know exactly what is expected of them. Rubrics are best coupled with examples of student work, providing concrete representations of expectations. Students can also benefit from filling out the rubrics themselves, engaging in their own self-assessment.

Prejournaling Exercise Rubric

- The student analyzes the issues in the court case.
- The student expresses feelings as a consumer.
- The student addresses the consequences of product superiority claims and connects to evidence.
- The student uses proper spelling, writing, and grammatical conventions.

Postjournaling Exercise Rubric

- The student's analysis of the experimental results explicitly cites the information in the data tables.
- The student discusses implications for fertilizing the garden, based on both experimental results and information from product ingredient research.
- The student reflects back on the Scotts v. TerraCycle case.
- The student reflects on the idea of *informed* consumer choice and contrasts it with flashy advertising and brand-recognition.
- The student uses proper spelling, writing, and grammatical conventions.

Helpful Tips

- Even though we are using our school garden as a backdrop for this experiment, it is not necessary to have a school garden. After the first time we performed this experiment, we determined that a more consistent light source was necessary. During the school year that followed, we constructed light boxes, based on

(Continued)

(Continued)

a Wisconsin Fast Plants model (see Web site). They are simple and inexpensive to construct and would be suitable in any classroom.

- Any forms of fertilizer could be used. We used Scotts MiracleGro because it was the company featured in the NPR broadcast, but any conventional fertilizer could work. The only criterion I would suggest is that there is a Material Safety Data Sheet (MSDS) available. Alternatives to worm compost could also be used, such as compost piles, hot piles, or even TerraCycle itself. The point is to introduce students to the idea of informed consumer choice, as opposed to being at the mercy of brand-recognition and advertising.

- A cross-curriculum project can be developed by having students in chemistry classes analyze the soil in each treatment, using colorimetric and pH probes from Vernier. They can report their findings to the field biology class, thus exercising community and collaborative skills, a major part of the scientific process.

10. My Life on a Podcast

Shane McKay
San Antonio, Texas

Recommended Level: Grades 10–12

Overall Objective: The learner will use technology to demonstrate a thorough understanding of microscopic life inside the human body. In addition, students will portray how each body system works to maintain homeostasis through first-person accounts using the lens of a microorganism, virus, or a body cell.

Standards Met (Texas Essential Knowledge and Skills for High School Biology § 112.34 [2010—2011]):

(c) Knowledge and skills.

> (4) Science concepts: The student knows that cells are the basic structures of all living things with specialized parts that perform specific functions and that viruses are different from cells. The student is expected to
>
>> (A) compare and contrast prokaryotic and eukaryotic cells;
>>
>> (B) investigate and explain cellular processes, including homeostasis, energy conversions, transport of molecules, and synthesis of new molecules; and
>>
>> (C) compare the structures of viruses to cells, describe viral reproduction, and describe the role of viruses in causing diseases such as human immunodeficiency virus (HIV) and influenza.
>
> (10) Science concepts: The student knows that biological systems are composed of multiple levels. The student is expected to
>
>> (A) describe the interactions that occur among systems that perform the functions of regulation, nutrient absorption, reproduction, and defense from injury or illness in animals;
>>
>> (B) describe the interactions that occur among systems that perform the functions of transport, reproduction, and response in plants; and
>>
>> (C) analyze the levels of organization in biological systems and relate the levels to each other and to the whole system.
>
> (11) Science concepts: The student knows that biological systems work to achieve and maintain balance. The student is expected to:
>
>> (A) describe the role of internal feedback mechanisms in the maintenance of homeostasis; and
>>
>> (C) summarize the role of microorganisms in both maintaining and disrupting the health of both organisms.[1]

Materials Needed:

- iPod or any MP3 device with recording capabilities (16 GB or higher)
- A computer
- Griffin iTalk (for iPod), or a USB headset microphone (for computer), or any recording device that attaches to an MP3
- iTunes
- GarageBand software (for Mac users)
- Audacity software (for PC users)

In this lesson, students explore how microscopic organisms survive, move, communicate, and reproduce inside the human body by writing a first-person account of a cell inside the body. The learner will then use these writings to establish a narrative and create a podcast that can be hosted on the Web through the school's Web site, a teacher's Web site, or some other free hosting Web site.

This project is most effective when students work in pairs and have ample time to research and prepare their podcast. Furthermore, this can be turned into a class assignment, with the establishment of teams that will write a section of the narrative and read their storyline to the class. The class decides which narrative sections need improvement, propose changes, and approve storylines that are ready for publication.

The largest portion of this project is writing and editing the narrative. Students must have basic research and writing skills in order to be successful. Science teachers may find it useful to create a cross-curricular connection with the English department while working on the writing and editing of the project.

The following are steps to follow to create the narrative and podcast:

1. Pass out the student guidelines for the narrative (see Figure 10.1) and review them with the class. Then pass out the scoring rubric (see Figure 10.2). By doing this, you are setting the scoring criteria and expectations for the project.

(Text continues on page 57)

Figure 10.1   Guidelines: My Life on a Podcast

You and a partner will be creating a podcast on the day and the life of a cellular organism that is either located in the human body or could invade the human body. This will be a first person account of where you come from, where you are going, what you are seeing, and what are you doing. Remember to use *I, me, we,* and *us,* since this is a first person account. Be as vivid and real as possible and consider your surroundings. (What does it look like, sound like, feel like, and taste like?) Draw in your audience by painting a mental picture of your life as a cell. Enjoy the creative side of this assignment while continuing to be conscientious about important scientific information. It is important that you make sure your project is completely accurate, well organized, research based, clever, high in quality, and correctly formatted.

You and your partner can choose one of the following topics (if you would like to choose something different, please come and ask me):

Topics

Red blood cell	Food molecule
White blood cell (T-Lymphocyte)	H_2O molecule
Platelet	Virus
O_2 molecule	Bacteria
CO_2 molecule	Cancer cell
Skin cell	Other: _____

Once you have agreed on a topic, follow these guidelines in writing your narrative. Be sure to include all of the specified information.

Research: Find as much information about that cell as you can. Where does it originate? How does it die? What is its purpose? How does it move or travel? Does it ever attack or get attacked? How does it obtain energy and get rid of waste, or does it even do that? Does it reproduce? Let the research guide you. The more detail you include, the better the podcast will be.

(Continued)

Figure 10.1 (Continued)

Introduction: Name, role, background information. Where are you from? What do you do? Do you have any relatives?

Act 1—Origins: How did you begin? What do you see? How are you moving? What's around you? Did you evolve or were you always this way? What's your destination? Do you have a purpose in this body you're in?

Act 2—Explain your journey: What systems are you passing through? What are you smelling, tasting, touching, feeling, seeing, doing? Do you get attacked? Are you going through any type of transformation?

Act 3—Your destination: What is your end result? How was your day? Did it take long? What did you do? How is your day going to end? And tomorrow? How much longer will you live? How will you die, or will you ever die? If you die, how will your body process you out?

Bibliography: Make sure you correctly cite your sources of information—author, year, publisher, city, state, pages, and so on—at the end of your podcast. This also gives you an opportunity to thank anyone who helped you on your assignment or gave support.

Figure 10.2 Grading Rubric: My Life on a Podcast

Concept	4	3	2	1	Score
Content Accuracy	Completely accurate: all facts were precise and explicit; covered topic in depth with details and examples; subject knowledge was excellent	Mostly accurate; a few inconsistencies or errors in information; included essential knowledge about the topic	Somewhat accurate; more than a few inconsistencies or errors in information; included essential information with one or two factual errors	Completely inaccurate; the facts in this project were misleading to the audience; content was minimal and or there were several factual errors	
Ideas	Ideas were easy to understand and well developed	Ideas were clear and easy to understand	Ideas were somewhat unclear and need some explanation	Ideas were hard to understand and often confusing	
Organization	Extremely well organized; logical easy-to-follow format; flowed smoothly from one idea to the other; cleverly conveyed; organization enhanced the effectiveness	Presented in a thoughtful manner; there were signs of organization and most transitions were easy to follow, but at times ideas were unclear	Somewhat organized; ideas were not presented coherently and transitions were not always smooth, which at times distracted the audience	Choppy and confusing; format was difficult to follow; transition of ideas was abrupt and seriously distracted the audience	

(Continued)

Figure 10.2 (Continued)

Concept	4	3	2	1	Score
Research	Went above and beyond to research information; brought in personal ideas and information to enhance project; used a variety of resources to include (Internet, publications, interviews, three or more sources)	Did a very good job of researching; used a variety of resources (used only one to two sources)	Used one type of resource	Did not utilize resources effectively; did little or no fact gathering	
Creativity	Was extremely clever and presented with originality; a unique approach that truly enhanced the project (vivid details were given that made it come alive)	Was clever at times; thoughtfully and uniquely presented (some details given but did not come alive)	Added a few original elements to enhance the project, but not incorporated throughout (very few details given)	Little creative energy used during this project; was bland, predictable, and lacked any zip	
Quality	Final product was complete and accurate; contained added elements that enhanced the project (music, background sounds, etc.)	Final product was complete and accurate; it was appealing but lacked a few added elements	Final product was complete but limited in detail and effort	Final product was incomplete, missed key parts, and or lacked effort	
Totals					

(Continued from page 52)

2. Students write the narrative. This establishes a great opportunity to create a cross-curricular connection with the English department. Make a proposal to an English teacher about the writing portion of this assignment to see if they would be willing to partner with you in this assignment. Your students would benefit by writing the narrative in their English class. After it is written, students need to work on reading the narrative out loud and practice enunciation.

3. Once the narrative is in place, the class (if a class assignment) or the team (if done in small groups) selects a broadcaster for their podcast. The broadcaster then must practice reading the narrative out loud many times and work on the enunciation of words, speech deliverance, and cadence. Furthermore, it is helpful if students from an advanced speech class can work with the broadcasters and coach them.

4. Upon the completion of rehearsals, the teams can begin recording their podcast. Each group either works with their MP3 device or iPod using the Griffin iTalk attached. If using a PC, it is recommended that students use a USB headset microphone. Furthermore, if students are using a PC, it is highly recommended that they use Audacity (free software from Windows) to record and edit their podcast. For Mac users, it is recommended that they use GarageBand software as an editing tool.

5. After each section has been recorded and downloaded onto the computer, it is time to edit their production. If the recordings are not in proper order, it is important to get each section in the proper position. The teams may choose to add music to the background and delete any sections that are not clear. Some editing programs do not allow you to add background music, so check before you begin editing.

6. When the production is complete, it is time to upload the file onto iTunes. If using Audacity for the PC, the file must be exported and converted into an MP3 file. Next, students may open up iTunes and import the file.

7. At this point, you may either choose to publish the podcasts online or grade the projects using the rubrics. Usually, it works best to grade all the projects first and then post the projects on the Web.

Helpful Tips

- It works best when students have the opportunity to record one section at a time. When the teams get to the editing phase, the listener will have no idea that each section was recorded separately.
- You should take into account the duration of the podcast. Podcasts that are five to seven minutes are a good length.
- It is also best to record the introduction after the completion of the additional sections. This permits each team to record exactly what will be on the podcast and set the stage for an exciting adventure.
- Teams benefit greatly if they have the opportunity to record their segments at home. They are able to rehearse more times and be in a quieter work area to concentrate and focus. If this is not an option, try the library.
- When teams decide to add music to the podcast, it is important that they use podsafe music. This is music that can be legally downloaded and used as background music. There are numerous podsafe music sites for you and your students to use. Music adds an element of suspense, intrigue, and action.
- If you are going to post the podcasts on the Web, your Web server must support RSS feeds. Talk to your district technology person for further information and details.

Note

1. From *Chapter 112. Texas Essential Knowledge and Skills for Science Subchapter C. High School: §112.34. Biology,* by the Texas Education Agency. Retrieved April 1, 2010, from http://ritter.tea.state.tx.us/rules/tac/chapter112/ch112c.html

℞ 11. Getting the Dirt on Soil

J-Petrina McCarty-Puhl
Reno, Nevada

Recommended Level: Grades 10–12

Overall Objective: In self-directed investigations, students will learn about different types and characteristics of soils and their formation.

Standards Met (Nevada): Students know that soil, derived from weathered rocks and decomposed organic material, is found in layers. Describe the structure of soil, its components, and how it is formed.

Materials Needed:

- A small plastic bag of soil brought by each student from his or her yard
- Metric rulers
- Munsell soil color book
- Crayons
- Graduated cylinders
- Calgon
- Distilled water
- pH color chart
- Universal indicator
- Petri dishes
- Grease pencils
- Drawing paper
- Handheld black light
- Electronic balance or scales
- Stereomicroscopes or hand magnifiers
- Forceps
- Test tubes
- Test tube racks
- Magnets
- Area map
- Small graduated cylinders

Soil can be important evidence at a crime scene because it is easily and inadvertently transferred. Like other trace evidence, the forensic examination of soil involves a comparison of samples in order to establish a link or relationship: The more characteristics that can be matched, the greater the probability of common origin. Low-power microscopy can lead into mineralogy and the refraction of light; overall characteristics of soil can be related to geological processes and geography. Comparative analysis uses physical properties such as density, magnetism, and particle size, as well as chemical properties, such as pH. Students are also asked to determine the locations of the soils on a city map.

At the end of this unit, students should be able to understand the following:

- Why soils are class evidence
- When soils can be used as circumstantial evidence
- How to present data mathematically using graphs
- How to identify soil's common constituents
- How to relate soil type to different biomes

Following are directions to students for the various activities that comprise this unit:

Activity 1

- Bring a soil sample to school. It should be in a zip-top bag labeled with your name, date collected, and the specific location.
- All of your observations and investigations are designed to help you describe your sample in the most detailed fashion possible. *All observations are to be recorded in your notebook in an organized fashion.*
- Compare the color of the soil sample to the color chart in the Munsell color book. Determine the letter-number combination of the color that best matches your sample and record it in your notebook.
- Using hand lenses and the binocular microscope, discover the variety of materials found in your sample and list them. It is not a list with percentages or numbers, but an accurate, detailed list of the variety of things found in your sample. This list might include seeds, sand particles, roots, insects, and so on.
- Place a small amount of your sample in a Petri dish and allow it to dry with the lid off overnight. (Place the lid with your name on it under the dish.)
- Based on your initial investigation and inventory of your soil, define soil.

Soil is one of the most common materials in the world. The three major components of soil are sand, silt, and clay. These major components determine a soil's properties. Sand is the end result of chemical and physical weathering of parent rock. Slow anaerobic decomposition of vegetative matter forms a dark organic soil, such as that found in swamps and bogs. The composition of soil varies from place to place and is controlled by five important factors: climate, parent material, living organisms, topography, and time. A sample taken a few meters deep may have a composition very different from a sample taken above it. A similar result can occur when samples are taken a few meters apart. This variability can sometimes be used to conclusively point to a common origin.

The forensic definition of soil includes any artifacts mixed in with the soil, such as fragments of glass, cinders, asphalt, paint, metal, concrete, bricks, and so on, as well as natural products. Often, it is the presence of artifacts that makes a soil sample unique to a particular location, thereby providing a link to another sample. For example, soil from either side of a galvanized fence usually contains zinc; dirt below an asphalt shingle roof may show shingle stones; potting soils often contain slow-release fertilizer tablets.

Soil can be important physical evidence at a crime scene because it is everywhere and is easily and accidentally transferred (remember the Locard's Exchange Principle). Samples of soil or mud can provide association between a suspect's car, clothing, shoes, or other items used or found at a crime scene. As with most forensic physical evidence, the tests are comparative in order to determine a common origin.

Activity 2

- Direct ultraviolet light on the soil sample. Note which particles fluoresce, if any. Certain minerals, such as fluorite, calcite, and willemite, as well as many manufactured articles, such as fibers, plastics, and paper, will also fluoresce.
- Pass a magnet through the soil to collect and identify any iron that might be present.
- The color of the soil is generally related to the presence of particular minerals or organic matter. Red soils are associated with highly oxidized iron, black soils with organic matter. Wet soil is usually darker than dry soil.
- Using crayons or colored pencils, reproduce as closely as possible the color of your sample in your notebook. . . . Smearing wet soil onto your paper does NOT count!
- To determine the pH of your soil sample, place a small amount of the sample in a test tube. Add about a centimeter of distilled water and shake it with your thumb over the open end of the tube. Let it settle, and note any discoloration of the water. Then add a drop of Universal indicator. Compare the solution to the color chart at your instructor's desk and record the pH.

Activity 3

- The composition of soil not only determines the color of the soil but also the range of particle sizes (texture). Compare the sizes of your soil particles using a metric ruler. Randomly pick 10 particles and measure their diameters. Add them together and take an average.
- Prepare a comparison of your particle sizes to the data from five other members of the class. This should be done in a visible, graphic fashion.
- If two soils are from the same location, they should contain particles of similar densities. To determine the density of a small amount of your soil, measure a set volume of soil and then weigh it. Remember that density is equal to mass divided by volume.

Activity 4

- To determine the sand, silt, and clay composition of your soil sample, you will find out how quickly the soil particles settle and the suspension in the water clears.

  1. Place 30 milliliters (mL) of dry soil into a 100-mL graduated cylinder. Add 2 mL of Calgon solution, and fill the cylinder with water to the 90-mL mark. Cap the cylinder with your hand, and shake the graduated cylinder for two minutes to thoroughly mix the sample.

  2. Place the cylinder on the table and wait for 40 seconds. Measure the volume of material that has settled to the bottom of the cylinder. That is the column of sand that is present in your sample.

  3. After 30 minutes have passed, measure again. This measurement should be taken between the upper surface of the sand and the top of the silt. Silt particles are lighter and smaller than sand and settle out more slowly. Calculate the amount of silt present in your sample.

  4. Your sample needs to rest overnight. Take the measurement from the top of the silt to the surface of the material that settled overnight. This is the volume of clay in your sample.

Activity 5

- On the city map for your class, you are to place a number that identifies your sample as unique. Your class is to create a coded list for all of the soil samples as a key to the map.
- Place a small amount of soil in your hand. Get it wet and roll the soil between your fingers. Describe the texture and feel. Is it gritty, sticky, slick, or spongy?
- What materials in soil might place it near each of the following locations?

Highway	Ranch
Home	River
Commercial building	Gas station
School	Railroad track
Ocean	Forest
Garden	Volcano

Activity 6

- Why is sand not useful as soil evidence?
- Glass and sand are composed mainly of _____. How could you tell them apart?
- Earthworms digest organic matter, recycle nutrients, and make the surface soil richer. One earthworm can digest 36 tons of soil in one year. Summarize the article on soil formation.
- Read and summarize the Coors kidnapping article.

Helpful Tips

- This series of activities is targeted for my forensic science students at the high school level, but it could easily be broken into separate sections for younger students.
- This activity is an excellent way to review such concepts as density, pH, and settling rates.

(Continued)

(Continued)

■ After collecting all the data, a class chart is made that compares the density of soils from around the city. We also locate all the different soil samples on a topographic map of the region.

■ To engage students, I include articles on crimes where soil evidence has played an important role, such as in Adolph Coors's kidnapping.

■ I let students work on different activities of the unit at the same time because many of the materials are limited in number. The students must determine what they have to accomplish and plan their time accordingly.

▧ 12. Water Purification

Chris Dodds
Greenfield, Ohio

Recommended Level: Grades 9–12

Overall Objective: Students will develop an understanding of the application of water purification technologies, their effects on the environment, and the current innovative design ideas for improving water technologies in the world today.

Standards Met (National Technology):

The Nature of Technology: Students will develop an understanding of the characteristics and scope of technology; Students will develop an understanding of the core concepts of technology; Students will develop an understanding of the relationships among technologies and the connections between technology and other fields of study.

Technology and Society: Students will develop an understanding of the effects of technology on the environment.

Abilities for a Technological World: Students will develop abilities to assess the impact of products and systems.

The Designed World: Students will develop an understanding of and be able to select and use agricultural and related biotechnologies.[1]

Materials Needed:

- *Water* (DVD)
- Containers
  - Used 12 oz water bottle
  - Three 8 oz plastic cups and rubber bands
- Contaminates
  - 1 tbs sawdust
  - 1 tbs sweeper lint

- 1 tbs Styrofoam
- 1 tbs soil

- Cleaners
  - Window screen
  - Coffee filter
  - Brown paper towel
  - Computer paper

This four-day project was developed to stress the importance of clean water in sustaining our environment and promoting our health. Students draw on their multiple intelligences in hands-on learning activities. In developing this project, I enjoyed the collaboration of Mike Honnold, lead operator in charge of the water treatment plant in Coshocton, Ohio.

Day 1: The Importance of a Clean Water Supply

Introduce facts related to the lack of clean drinking water world-wide and discuss them with the students:

- 1.1 billion people lack access to clean drinking water.
- Nearly 2 million people die each year due to waterborne-related disease, 90% of whom are children under the age of 5. Every 8 seconds a child dies from water-related disease.
- The lack of clean drinking water is at the root of the African HIV/AIDS pandemic. Waterborne illness considered normally mild in healthy adults becomes an incurable death sentence for those affected by HIV/AIDS.

- In the United States, 900,000 illnesses are caused by contaminated drinking water, resulting in 900 deaths annually.
- By 2025, one in 800 million will be living in absolute water scarcity.
- The World Health Organization (WHO) has declared a worldwide water crisis among the world's poorest people.

Explain that in most third-world applications, the solution to the clean drinking water need is found in the concrete biosand filter. The biosand filter has the ability to produce safe, clean drinking water from both contaminated surface water and ground water sources.

Day 2: Local and National Filtration
Systems Affecting the World Water Supply

Show the DVD *Water* to explore current purification technologies and current design proposals related to world water issues. During the video, have the students complete the worksheet shown in Figure 12.1 to reinforce learning concepts.

Figure 12.1   *Water* DVD Worksheet (correct answers in italics)

Turn the tap on a surprisingly rich hour that explores the many mysteries of H_2O. Can new technology coax rain from the skies to help save drought-starved nations?

1. Name two hard materials that water can cut through. *Steel, Aluminum*

2. How many psi is the water jet? *87,000*

3. Name three advantages of using water in a cut? *Reusable, doesn't get dull, clean cut*

4. Water is made up of two parts _____ and one part _____. *Hydrogen, oxygen*

5. Water turns sunlight into _____ for plants. *Food*

6. The by-product of photosynthesis is _____. *Oxygen*

7. 80 percent of water in California crops is _____. *Irrigated*

8. _____ gallons of water to raise one apple. *25*

9. _____ gallons of water to raise one pound of meat. *1,200*

10. The Colorado River is responsible for _____ percent of US fresh produce. *25*

11. Hydro dams turn at _____ mph. *60*

12. _____ percent of our renewable electricity is from hydro dams. *24*

13. Water that turns into steam is called _____ energy. *Hydroelectric*

14. Steam takes up _____ more space than water. *1600%*

15. Steam engines used _____ gallons of water per 30 miles. *2,000*

16. Canada has _____ percent of the world's fresh water. *20*

17. _____ percent of the world's fresh water is stored in glaciers. *75*

18. _____ percent of the world's water is in the oceans. *97*

19. _____ is taking seawater and making it drinkable. *Desalinization*

20. In Orange County, California, _____ filters filter _____ gallons of water for drinking. *Micro, 70,000,000*

21. _____ are a natural form of water filter. *Aquifers*

22. _____ flares are shot into clouds to increase rain. *Rocket*

23. _____ percent increase in rain from seed clouds. *10*

Day 3: Water Purification Project

Working with a partner, have the students experiment with hands-on application of water biotechnologies. Students apply filtration techniques for removal of large particles versus smaller particulates, following the steps below:

1. Measure out 10 oz of water and pour into the used water bottle. Add 1 tbs of sawdust into the water.

2. Add 1 tbs of sweeper lint to the concoction.

3. Add 1 tbs of Styrofoam to the mixture.

4. Add 1 tbs of soil to the mixture.

5. Put the cap on the mixture. Shake well, but don't stir.

6. Place the screen on the first cup. Pour the mixture into the first cup until the cup is full.

7. Apply the coffee filter with a rubber band and pour.

8. Attach the paper towel to the top of the cup with a rubber band. Then pour the water through.

9. Apply the paper towel and pour into the next cup.

10. Make a cone filter out of the computer paper and attach to the cup with a rubber band. Pour the mixture into the cup.

11. Pour the water into the clean, unused cup and turn in to your instructor for a grade. You will be graded on following instructions and the clarity of water achieved.

Day 4: Summary of Project and Application to Future Careers

Engage the class in a discussion of the video and the hands-on application. Explore further concepts and proposals in water purification. Introduce potential careers in biotechnology relative to water purification. Have the students complete the 10-question quiz shown in Figure 12.2.

Figure 12.2   Water Purification Quiz (correct answers in italics)

True or false (circle answer)

1. Nearly 2 million people die each year due to waterborne-related disease. *True* False

2. The lack of clean drinking water is at the root of the African HIV/AIDS pandemic. *True* False

3. Every 8 days a child dies from water-related disease. True *False*

4. During a boiling alert, boiling the water always makes it safe for consumption. *True* False

5. A charcoal filter is sufficient for treating water from an unknown contaminate. True *False*

Short answer

6. Which particles were the easiest to separate from the dirty water during the experiment? Why?

7. What country has the freshest water? *Canada*

8. Name three common materials (used during the experiment) that are used to filter water? *Window screen, coffee filter, paper towel, computer paper*

9. Which filter removed the finest particles? *Computer paper*

10. Do you think a clean water supply will become more important or less important in the future? *Yes* Why?

Helpful Tips

- I suggest that you consult the Wikipedia article on water purification (found at http://en.wikipedia.org/wiki/Water_purification) for background information, and share it with your students.
- The following Web sites can be helpful in carrying out this project:

  http://www.acreativetouch.us/

  http://earthfirst.com/innovate-or-die-a-bike-makes-clean-water/

  http://iteaconnect.org/

  http://shop.history.com/detail.php?p=69839&v=All

  http://www.thirstrelief.org/news.htm

  http://www.youtube.com/watch?v=RWdf1ME3doE&feature=PlayList&p=4323412C7AD35D46&index=1

Note

1. Printed with permission of ITEA, www.iteaconnect.org

▧ 13. Atom-Building Bingo

Ann Shioji
San Jose, California

Recommended Level: Grade 9

Overall Objective: Students will use manipulatives to understand how protons, neutrons, and electrons determine the atom name.

Standards Met (National Science Content): Students understand the structure of atoms. Students have the abilities necessary to do scientific inquiry by using models.[1]

Materials Needed (per group of four students):

- 3 strings: one 6", one 10", and one 15" (representing orbitals)
- Periodic table
- Atom pieces (circles, can be game pieces or made of construction paper using a

0.5" diameter hole punch):
- 20 red circles (electrons)
- 20 yellow circles (neutrons)
- 20 blue circles (protons)
- Atom Bingo cards

Atoms are made of three main parts: positively charged protons, neutrons with no charge, and negatively charged electrons. Students must understand that protons and neutrons are found in the nucleus (the center of the atom) and electrons are found in orbitals around the nucleus. Manipulatives are a good way for students to communicate an understanding of this basic concept to the teacher and to others. In a group format, students can teach other students this concept. In addition, students who are normally not engaged by writing in science can be motivated by using these manipulatives in a game format so that the pressure of language is temporarily removed.

Students use the periodic table and information gathered in notes to figure out how the model should look. To participate in this activity, students need to know how to figure out the number of protons, neutrons, and electrons for each element. This includes the capacity of electrons for each orbital: the first orbital holds two electrons, the next two orbitals hold eight electrons each. Therefore, when you check the models for each group, you should ensure that this rule is followed. Also, you should check the number of neutrons. (The students should have previous knowledge that the atomic mass minus the number of protons results in the number of neutrons.) In addition, the number of protons should equal the number of neutrons. (See the Gifted/Advanced Adaptations in the Helpful Hints section that follows.)

Activity

- Divide the class into groups of four.
- Give each student an Atom Bingo card (see Figure 13.1), and instruct the students to write their names on the back.
- Have each group obtain the group materials: strings and atom pieces.
- Instruct them as follows:

  You have 20 protons (blue circles), 20 neutrons (yellow circles), and 20 electrons (red circles). You also have three orbitals. REMEMBER: The first orbital, closest to the nucleus, can only hold *two* electrons. The next two orbitals can hold eight electrons each. Build atoms of the elements listed on your Bingo card. Each atom is worth five points. The first group to be done with the entire card gets a surprise!

- When students have made their model of an element on their card, have them raise their hands, and then go check their model.
- If the model is correct, stamp the corresponding element on their Bingo cards, and have the students continue the activity with building an atom of another element.
- If the model is incorrect, tell the group to try again.
- When students are done, have them complete a reflection card (three facts they learned about atoms and a question they still have about atoms).

Figure 13.1   Sample Atom Bingo Card

H	He	Li	Be	B
C	N	O	F	Ne

H	He	Li	Be	B
C	N	O	F	Ne

H	He	Li	Be	B
C	N	O	F	Ne

H	He	Li	Be	B
C	N	O	F	Ne

H	He	Li	Be	B
C	N	O	F	Ne

H	He	Li	Be	B
C	N	O	F	Ne

H	He	Li	Be	B
C	N	O	F	Ne

H	He	Li	Be	B
C	N	O	F	Ne

H	He	Li	Be	B
C	N	O	F	Ne

H	He	Li	Be	B
C	N	O	F	Ne

H	He	Li	Be	B
C	N	O	F	Ne

H	He	Li	Be	B
C	N	O	F	Ne

HelpfulTips

- This activity is a good activity for English language learners. Students see other groups who understand the activity (once it gets going) and become more engaged if there is a contest. I will offer candy or another incentive for groups who complete the activity first. The students are also aware that each stamp they receive (you can punch the cards or initial them) is awarded a set amount of points. This way, students have a tangible consequence for completion of the activity.
- *Gifted/Advanced Adaptation:* You could demonstrate the first few atoms on the board. The students will have to figure out the pattern, and you can approve or deny the accurateness of the students' models until the students figure out the number of protons determines the atom. Also, the students can make common ions using these manipulatives.
- Blue and red were used to represent the positive and negative charges, respectively. However, if these colors are not available or are discouraged for use by your district, you can use whatever colors are available.
- A foam pad, such as that used for scrapbooking, is a good background to use for the orbitals if game pieces are used so that the pieces are not too slippery on the desk.
- Have the materials for each group pre-assembled in bags to make the activity go faster.

Note

1. Reprinted with permission from *National Science Education Standards,* 1996, by the National Academy of Sciences, courtesy of the National Academies Press, Washington, D.C.

14. Modéle: An Electron Configuration Experience

Jeffery R. Wehr
Odessa, Washington

Recommended Level: Grades 9–12

Overall Objective: Students will convey their knowledge regarding electron configuration and the four quantum numbers associated with the elements located within the periodic table.

Standards Met: Understand the atomic nature of matter and how it relates to physical and chemical properties and serves as the basis for the structure and use of the periodic table; Analyze the forms of energy in a system, subsystems, or parts of a system; Understand the structure of atoms, how atoms bond to form molecules, and that molecules form solutions; Analyze how physical, conceptual, and mathematical models represent and are used to investigate objects, events, systems, and processes.

Materials Needed:

- Periodic table
- Various materials specific to each student's discipline choice

Before this activity begins, your students should have a good understanding of electron configuration. Electron configuration was first conceived under the Bohr model of the atom, and it is still common to speak of shells and subshells even with the advances in understanding of the quantum-mechanical nature of electrons. The four quantum numbers describing the electron configuration of the elements should also have been introduced. Since electron configuration can be difficult to comprehend, I have found differentiated instruction to be a great avenue for students to express their understanding. Allowing students to choose a discipline they are interested in and aligning their concept of electron configuration to that discipline not only increases the student's chance of understanding the concept, but also incorporates modeling, one of the principal instruments of modern science.

The first quantum number (principal quantum number), n, is the energy level. It can have values of 1, 2, 3, and so on. The principal quantum number gives information about relative electron cloud size. The second quantum number, l, is the energy sublevel and can range in value from 0 to $(n - 1)$. It gives information about the shape of the electron cloud. A sublevel with $l = 0$ is an s sublevel, $l = 1$ is a p sublevel, $l = 2$ is a d sublevel, and $l = 3$ is an f sublevel. The third quantum number, m, gives information about the orientation in space of each orbital. The fourth quantum number, s, is the spin of the electron. Spin is either clockwise or counterclockwise and is designated $+\frac{1}{2}$ or $-\frac{1}{2}$.

Have your students choose an element depending on their level of chemistry knowledge. In an introductory chemistry course, I have the students choose no lower than the element potassium, ensuring that at least four energy levels are modeled. However, using elements with just two or three energy levels could easily be adapted and take less time. Each student should independently determine the electron configuration for his or her respective element and then choose a favorite discipline *besides* science. (I know this may be *extremely* difficult for you to imagine, but it just may be true.) Some examples my students have produced include poetry or acting skits (humanities), welding (industrial arts) or sculpting (fine arts), historical battle skits (social science), and financial statements or ledger books (business). One point to make very clear is that the student's expression or model should be somewhat evasive; if the student reveals the element or electron configuration so that other students immediately decipher their model, the investigation may become insincere.

Next, have your students begin with the first quantum number, the energy level. Depending on their choice of discipline, they need to somehow represent this number while remembering that the other quantum numbers need to intertwine with the discipline's theme. For example, a sculpture (fine arts) may utilize different physical levels in the sculpture to represent the first quantum number (low places on the sculpture would equal 1, the next highest part on the sculpture would equal 2), yet the student needs to think ahead to what the second quantum number will be. Since the second quantum number represents the energy sublevel (s, p, d, or f), the student could use different shapes to represent these energy sublevels. The third quantum number, the shape of the orbital and hence number of electrons within the orbital, could be represented by the grouping of the shapes within the sculpture. For example, since the s sublevel holds two electrons, two arrows grouped together on the sculpture could represent the second and third quantum numbers. Finally, the fourth quantum number is electron spin and could be represented by direction, and the orbital being empty or full could be represented by color. If the above model was placed all together, the completed sculpture would appear as shown in Figure 14.1. Can you determine which element this extremely simple work of art expresses?

Figure 14.1   Sculpture of the Electron Configuration of Scandium

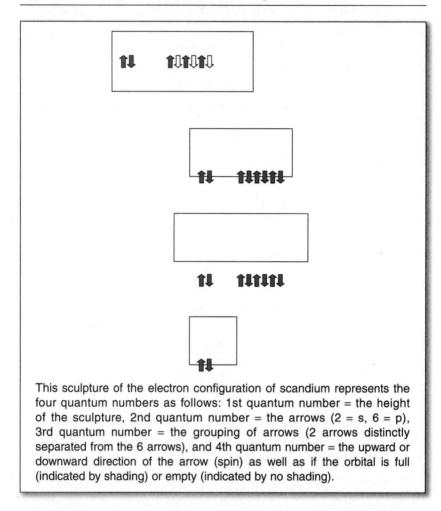

This sculpture of the electron configuration of scandium represents the four quantum numbers as follows: 1st quantum number = the height of the sculpture, 2nd quantum number = the arrows (2 = s, 6 = p), 3rd quantum number = the grouping of arrows (2 arrows distinctly separated from the 6 arrows), and 4th quantum number = the upward or downward direction of the arrow (spin) as well as if the orbital is full (indicated by shading) or empty (indicated by no shading).

Give your students one class period to choose their element (make sure no students choose the same element), choose their academic discipline, write the longhand and shorthand electron configuration for their chosen element, and begin a rough draft list of supplies or materials needed for their model or expression. Make it clear that each student needs to bring his materials to class the next period. Give your students one or two class periods to construct their model or expression. On the final day, either create a stage for the presentations or build a circular gallery with the desks in the room for each model to be presented. Pass out a grading rubric template to each student (see Figure 14.2).

Figure 14.2   Grading Rubric

Modéle: An Electron Configuration Experience

Name: _____

Overall Objective: To create a working model or expression (using any academic discipline) that conveys the quantum numbers that describe the electron configuration of a specific element.

Assignment: Walk around to each student's model or expression and write down the following information:

Name of student: _____

Title of model or expression: _____

Analysis of model or expression (**G**ood **F**air **P**oor):

Organization _____

Effort _____

Creativity _____

Interpretation:

Name the element represented _____

Explain how the 1st quantum number is represented.

Explain how the 2nd quantum number is represented.

Explain how the 3rd quantum number is represented.

Explain how the 4th quantum number is represented.

Write the longhand electron configuration: _____

Write the shorthand electron configuration: _____

If students are acting out a skit or reading a piece of literature they have created, have all other students gather as a group to determine the element (either collectively or individually). Otherwise, have each student use the grading rubric template and wander to all other models and determine all information from the grading rubric. For an added touch, I have provided hors d'oeuvres and sparkling cider for our events.

One class period is usually sufficient to view all of the models; once completed, we utilize a whole class period to discuss each project and confirm our predictions on which element each student was trying to model. In essence, the students convey their knowledge regarding electron configuration and the four quantum numbers associated with the elements located within the periodic table. Also, each student practices writing electron configuration each time he or she grades the other projects and can corroborate his or her understanding in group discussion. Allowing the students the choice of how to express this model aligns with differentiated instruction.

Helpful Tips

- This activity can easily be adapted to primary grade levels; use elements from the first two periods instead!
- The students should not share their element with the rest of the class so that, later, the other students can interpret the unknown element based on the presenter's model.
- Make sure no students choose the same element.
- Allow the students to be really creative; I have had many projects that originally made no sense, yet when performed or viewed as a finished model, really worked well!

 15. Remote Sensing

Jeffery R. Wehr
Odessa, Washington

Recommended Level: Grades 8–12

Overall Objective: Using technological devices, students will utilize the process of remote sensing to collect data from an unknown environment.

Standards Met:

Apply an understanding of direction, speed, and acceleration when describing the linear motion of objects; Analyze the patterns and arrangements of Earth systems and subsystems.

Analyze a variety of evidence, including rock formations or fossils, to construct a sequence of geologic events; Analyze the factors that influence weather and climate; Analyze why curiosity, honesty, cooperation, openness, and skepticism are important to scientific explanations and investigations; Analyze the scientific, mathematical, and technological knowledge, training, and experience needed for occupational/career areas of interest.

Materials Needed:

- Computer with video and audio input (laptop works best)
- Video capturing software (such as Adobe, Avid Video, FutureTel, In Sync, or Ulead)
- Remote-controlled vehicle
- Wireless remote camera, such as http://www.x10 .com/catalog/cat_cameras .htm (Remember to purchase the battery pack for complete wireless camera.)
- Various materials for the unknown environment. These items may include rock samples, remnants of life (shells, bones), remnants of intelligent life (forged metal, plastics), water samples, wind simulated by fans.
- Sheet (such as old bed linen)

Remote sensing is a technology for gathering information to interpret noncontiguous geospatial data from which to extract information about the surrounding environment. Remote sensing is used in a variety of applications—from probing fire danger by firemen to analyzing data from outer space. Anywhere humans either do not want to go (harsh environment) or cannot go (deep aspects of outer space) is ideal for remote sensing. I ask my students if they can provide examples of the use of remote sensing in their everyday life, and most students respond with examples such as auto mechanics and the probes that reach into the engine to analyze fuel mixtures or physicians and the probes that reach into our bodies (such as CAT or MRI scans). We then discuss that our bodily senses are really remote sensors for our brains: the eyes gather electromagnetic radiation, the ears gather acoustic vibrations, the fingertips gather temperature, and so on. No single sense actually interprets any of the data, but it provides a sensor outside the brain to gather the information. The brain is really the interpreter of the data!

When preparing for this activity, make sure the students are not allowed to observe the setup. With the supplies you have gathered, devise a passable route, keeping the following in mind: the terrain type (type of rock, using descriptors or exact rock type), possible climate (dry, wet, temperatures, wind, elements), any water in this environment (in any form), and any life that was/is in this environment (discuss what brings you to this conclusion). I usually buy a bag of soil and spread it around on the floor, then place different rock samples along the way. Next, I place other items around the room, such as water, ice cubes, fans for creating wind storms, fossils, or really anything I can think of that would make remote sensing interesting! I once used an electric football game with a towel on it and dirt to simulate seismic activity . . . the students picked it up visually and recorded it as a movie (*.MOV or *.AVI file) on the computer and also captured the sound it created on the camera.

Next, set up a mission control center in the room where you will have a computer linked to the input of the wireless camera. Create enough space so that a team of students can gather around the computer and see what the remote sensor is relaying to the computer. Take the bed sheet or large drop cloth and surround the mission control so that the students are not tempted to actually look at what the remote sensor is doing in real time. Attach the wireless camera to the top of the remote-controlled vehicle and test it to make sure that it is working. You can either adjust the camera angle for the students or allow the students to calibrate the video and audio at mission control prior to the actual remote sensing. If students need a refresher on computer skills, you could run a mock trial the day before to allow the students to become familiar with the software, the interface between the wireless camera and the computer, and driving the remote-controlled vehicle.

Once everything is working properly, place the remote sensing device somewhere in the environment and let the students begin. Place students into teams of your choice and allow each team time to traverse the unknown environment collecting audio and video data. Either have your students create their own data table to record the event or have them respond to a list of data items in a template you prepare. They should provide data about the environment's geophysical properties as follows:

- Terrain type (type of rock, using descriptors or exact rock type)
- Climate (dry, wet, temperatures, wind, elements)
- Water (in any form) and the implications of what that means about pressure and temperature in the environment
- Life (Have your students discuss what brings them to this conclusion; one time I had a hamster roaming around in the environment!)
- Any unusual properties (Allow the students to interpret any ideas you had not thought of.)

Require the students to capture pictures from the video feed using the software and to attach any and all photographs printed during their experiment, making sure they label them correctly and estimate the scale (in centimeters or meters).

After all of the teams have completed their mission, have them join in a group discussion to ascertain the environment collectively. Allow them to defend the characteristics based on the data and pictures they collected. Allow the teams to analyze each other's data to help support their claims. In closing, you can either allow the students to walk through the environment or not; both choices have their pros and cons. If the students are mature enough, they will understand that the point of remote sensing is to collect data from a place that humans may never travel; even though we have collected a lot of data from the sun, humans will probably never get to go there. However, it can be educational and fun for the students to check their explanations against the reality of the environment too. If time allows, I usually follow up with a quick set of questions, such as the following:

1. Define remote sensing.

2. Which planets have we landed on and analyzed by remote systems?

3. Which planets have we sensed by remote systems without landing?

4. Provide ON EARTH examples of remote sensing.

5. How would you improve your remote sensing device for the environment in this laboratory?

6. How would you improve your remote sensing device for an underwater environment?

This lesson is a great way to incorporate technology in the classroom, while providing students with a practical, inquiry-based activity regarding remote sensing.

Helpful Tips

- Video files typically end with the extensions .avi, .mpg, .mov, .moov, .movie, or .qt. Check your editing software to see what kinds of file formats it accepts.
- When one team is operating the remote sensor, have the other team(s) planning for when it is their turn. This way, when a new team operates the remote sensor, the environment is new to them. However, any team that has already probed the environment is welcome to observe the rest of the teams as they operate the sensor.
- Although the wireless camera may be a little pricey, it can be used for a variety of applications in other classes or lessons—just be creative!

Teaching Math

Overview, Chapters 16–21

16. **Amy Maxey**, a math teacher in Winston-Salem, North Carolina, uses the trends in popularity of baby names over time to have students learn to construct a scatter plot. Then they describe the rate of change for a name's popularity.

17. **Cindy Couchman**, a math teacher in Buhler, Kansas, begins a lesson on box and whisker plots by having her students watch an explanation on the computer. Then they collect data from the Internet, use their graphing calculators to calculate quartiles, and use flip cameras to capture the hand-drawn plot, which they will transfer to a summary report of the data.

18. **Amy Maxey** offers a second lesson in which she develops a hypothetical experience for her students. They each select an animal-trainer occupation and then calculate the distances that their animal has traveled in a maze. The students use the Pythagorean theorem and explore the differences between Euclidean distance and non-Euclidean distances.

19. **Cindy Couchman** presents a second lesson in which she engages her students with a practical application of algebra. Working in small groups, they create a solar cooker from a box by cutting out a parabola on each side. They have to write the equation for the parabola using their graphing calculator, find the focus of the parabola, and construct their cooker using the parabola and focus points. The students enjoy testing their cookers with marshmallows or hot dogs!

20. **Ken Petersen**, a math teacher in Mountain View, Wyoming, guides his pre-calculus students to discover different sequences and

series from Pascal's triangle. This lesson uses the rows, row sums, diagonals, and diagonal sums.

21. **Ken Petersen**, in a second lesson, shows that in-class water-rocket launches enable his students to enhance their knowledge of parabolas in standard form, trigonometry, triangle properties, and correlation coefficients. Most important, students develop a love for higher-level math.

16. Mathematical Trends and Baby Names

Amy Maxey
Winston-Salem, North Carolina

Recommended Level: Grades 8–9

Overall Objective: Students will construct a scatter plot for the popularity of baby names over time and describe the rate of change for the name's popularity.

Standards Met (National Council of Teachers of Mathematics):

Algebra: Use mathematical models to represent and understand quantitative relationships; Draw reasonable conclusions about a situation being modeled; Analyze change in various contexts; Approximate and interpret rates of change from graphical numerical data.[1]

Materials Needed:

- Skittles
- Computer with Internet access
- Handout: Mathematical Trends and Baby Names

- Graph paper (optional) so students may construct patterns with Skittles on their desk

In this activity, students use Skittles (candy) to make scatter plots for the name ranking data found on the Social Security Web site (www.socialsecurity.gov). The names on the Web site are ranked by popularity for each year since 1890. Students find the popular trend for their own name or a name of their choice on the Web site and discuss its pattern of change with their small group. They use the Skittles to model the rates of change for the names over a period of time. The patterns are linear and nonlinear.

My strategy in the problem-based learning activity is to promote a student-centered problem-solving environment, rather than a teacher-centered one. The student-centered environment develops students as independent thinkers and learners and encourages them to collaborate with their peers. I plan the activity so that each student can contribute, despite their varying levels of mathematical knowledge.

My goal is for students to communicate mathematics. In the baby name activity, I strategically design prompt questions for students to discuss with their small group. For example:

- What names have increased or decreased in popularity?
- Are some names consistently popular?
- What makes a name popular?
- Do different cultures have different popular names? Explain.
- Do people have the same names in various regions of the world?
- Can one associate a name with a time period?

The questions encourage students to think about and to share the popularity or uniqueness of their own name and its cultural significance. It is important for students to appreciate and respect one another's differences. During their conversations, students entertain the idea of living in a different time period and whether the pattern of popularity for their name would change. The intent is to engage students in an informal conversation so they intuitively connect popular trends of names to linear or nonlinear patterns of change. Students will likely verbalize key mathematical concepts such as increasing, decreasing, and zero rate of change. Following are the steps to carry out the activity:

1. Distribute a small cup of Skittles to each student.

2. Have the students go to the Social Security Web site (www.social security.gov). Allow time for students to become familiar with the Web site.

3. Ask the students to locate their own name and model its popularity trend with Skittles.

4. Have the group describe and discuss the pattern that the scatter plot illustrates. Together, they should think about what type of equation could model the popularity trend. For example, is the trend linear or does it posses a curve?

5. Tell the students to find names with positive and/or negative popularity trends. They should record the names in a chart and describe their pattern over time.

Helpful Tips

- The Skittle scatter plot is a clear method for visual learners to "see" patterns and a technique to engage kinesthetic learners.
- The scatter plot made of Skittles on the students' desks will allow you to quickly assess their graph and to provide feedback.
- Students may struggle with verbalizing rates of change. Some helpful phrases to share are
  - Increases/decreases at a constant rate
  - Increases at an increasing rate
  - Increases at a decreasing rate
  - Decreases at an increasing rate
  - Decreases at a decreasing rate
  - The rate of change is zero

Note

1. Adapted with permission from *Principles and Standards for School Mathematics,* copyright © 2000 by the National Council of Teachers of Mathematics. All rights reserved.

17. Box and Whisker Plot Extravaganza

Cindy Couchman
Buhler, Kansas

Recommended Level: Grades 8–9

Overall Objective: Students will create their own box and whisker plot utilizing the technology of the computer, digital camera, and graphing calculator. Students will also have to summarize and interpret their data.

Standards Met:

National Council of Teachers of Mathematics: Instructional programs should enable all students to formulate questions that can be addressed with data and to collect, organize, and display relevant data to answer them; select and use appropriate statistical methods to analyze data; develop and evaluate inferences and predictions that are based on data; understand and apply basic concepts of probability.[1]

Kansas: The student collects, organizes, displays, explains, and interprets numerical (rational numbers) and non-numerical data sets in a variety of situations, with a special emphasis on measures of central tendency, by using box and whisker plots.

Materials Needed:

- Computer to access Internet and write a summary
- Graphing calculator
- Digital camera
- Large sheet of graph paper
- Worksheets

In this project for Algebra I, students are assigned a partner and a computer. The partners go to the Web site http://www.onlinemathlearning .com/box-plot.html and watch an explanation on box and whisker plots. Then, using the information from the video, they fill out a worksheet according to the following instructions:

Activity 1

After viewing the video tutorial, answer the following questions:

1. How are box and whisker plots helpful?

2. Box and whisker plots are based upon which measure of central tendency (mean, median, mode, range)?

3. What fraction of the data is contained in each quartile?

4. The second quartile is another name for the _____?

5. T or F The data must be in order to construct a box and whisker plot.

6. How many pieces of information are given in a box and whisker plot?

7. A piece of data that falls well outside the range of the other data is called an _____?

Answers can be found at http://regentsprep.org/REgents/math/ALGEBRA/AD3/boxwhisk.htm.

In the second part of the project, students use statistics found on the ESPN Web site to set up and create a box and whisker plot by hand, as follows:

Activity 2

1. Go to http://sports.espn.go.com/ncb/teams and select a team. For that team, go to statistics and to the 2007–2008 season. Select a player that played in that year and find their scoring outputs for every game that year (under game log).

2. With the data, set up and create a box and whisker plot.

3. Make an extra copy of the box and whisker plot and then switch one copy with another group.

4. From the two box and whisker plots, compare the two players and write an article about your comparisons. Be sure to mention highs, lows, and spread of scores.

5. Take a picture of both box and whisker plots using a digital camera and paste them into your document.

Note

1. Adapted with permission from *Principles and Standards for School Mathematics*, copyright © 2000 by the National Council of Teachers of Mathematics. All rights reserved.

⧜ 18. Maze Madness

Amy Maxey
Winston-Salem, North Carolina

Recommended Level: Grades 7–9

Overall Objective: Students will use the Pythagorean theorem to find and compare distances of hypothetical animals running through a maze.

Standards Met (National Council of Teachers of Mathematics):

Geometry: Represent problem situations with geometric models; apply geometric properties and relationships, including the Pythagorean theorem, to solve problems.[1]

Materials Needed:

- Graph paper
- Handout: Maze Madness

Students begin this geometry activity by completing the first part of the Maze Madness handout (see Figure 18.1)—an adventure paragraph to determine their occupations. For each occupation offered as an option, the career person uses a maze to train animals. Using the second part of the handout, students plot and connect coordinates consecutively to make segments that represent pathways in a maze. In the first maze, the pathways are horizontal and vertical, but in the second maze the pathways are diagonal.

Figure 18.1   Maze Madness

Maze Madness

I. Fill in the blanks with one of the choices or parts of speech.

I am a _____ and
zoo trainer, neuroscientist, veterinarian, psychologist

I am training a/an _____ to _____. In order to
animal   *verb*

command the _____ 's obedience, I will lead the animal
same animal

through two mazes. The maze consists of horizontal and vertical

movements. When the _____ gets to the end of the maze,
same animal

it will be rewarded with a/an _____ .
prize

II. Start at the origin and graph the following coordinates according to the compass direction. Draw segments to denote the path the animal travels in the maze. Do all work on a separate sheet of graph paper.

(Continued)

Figure 18.1 (Continued)

A→B: 4 units North

B→C; 3 units East

C→D; 6 units North

D→E; 8 units West

E→F; 5 units South

F→G; 5 units West

G→H; 5 units South

H→I; 12 units East

I→J; 3 units South

J→K; 4 units West

The _____ traveled _____ but would have traveled
    same animal   *total distance*

_____ if it had gone directly from Point A to the prize at
length of AK

Point K.

If the _____ eats _____ it will gain amazing
    same animal   *vegetable*

strength and will be able to break through secret passageways that allow

it to go from Point A to C, from C to E, and so on. Draw the described

segments on your graph, and then find their length.

AC = _____ , CE= _____ , EG = _____ , GI = _____ , IK = _____

Reflection Questions

1. Describe how you calculated the lengths in the first maze.

2. Explain how you found lengths in the second maze.

3. Name two triangles that have corresponding sides in the ratio of 2:1.

4. Name triangles that have congruent corresponding sides.

5. Name an isosceles triangle.

6. In your opinion, should animals be trained? Why or why not?

7. What is the purpose of training animals for the profession you chose?

Through this activity, students gain further understanding of vertical and horizontal change. The change in x and y values in the coordinate plane determine the side lengths for a right triangle. Vertical and horizontal change is also used in the slope formula. Students discover that each diagonal shortcut for the second maze is the hypotenuse of a right triangle. The length of the hypotenuse is found by using the Pythagorean Theorem. The length of the hypotenuse is shorter than the sum of the two legs of the triangle. This application is true for all triangles: The sum of two sides of a triangle is always greater than the third side. Students will identify congruent, similar, and isosceles triangles in the second maze.

Progressing through the handout, students reflect on their construction:

- They describe how they calculated horizontal and vertical lengths. Guide students to develop mathematical notation for vertical and horizontal change. For example, horizontal change is $x_2 - x_1$.
- They explain how they used vertical and horizontal lengths to calculate oblique lengths. Throughout the process of comparing and explaining vertical, horizontal, and oblique lengths, students communicate the Pythagorean theorem in their own words.
- Students identify similar and congruent triangles from their construction. In addition, they classify triangles as scalene, isosceles, or equilateral.

Helpful Tips

- Students should have prior knowledge of the Pythagorean theorem when completing this activity.
- The process of constructing the maze may be difficult for some students. In order to check for understanding, students can communicate the directions in their own words.
- Some students oppose the idea of training animals, whereas some view animal training as beneficial for future developments. Allow time for students to express their thoughts on this topic.
- After completing this lesson, students may determine whether or not they would enjoy a career with animals and develop an opinion on animal training.

Note

1. Adapted with permission from *Principles and Standards for School Mathematics,* copyright © 2000 by the National Council of Teachers of Mathematics. All rights reserved.

▨   19. Parabolic Solar Cooker

Cindy Couchman
Buhler, Kansas

Recommended Level: Grades 10–12

Overall Objective: Students will apply the quadratic regression feature of the graphing calculator, the table feature of the calculator, and their knowledge of the focus point to create a slow cooker from a box.

Standards Met:

National Council of Teachers of Mathematics: Algebra: The student shall understand and compare the properties of classes of functions, including exponential, polynomial, rational, logarithmic, and periodic functions.[1]

Kansas: The student represents, generates, and/or solves real-world problems that involve distance and two-dimensional geometric figures, including parabolas in the form $ax^2 + c$.

Materials Needed:

- Boxes
- Box cutter knife (or cutting tool of some sort)
- Aluminum foil
- Wire
- Food to test—hot dogs or marshmallows
- Graphing calculator
- Ruler
- Poster board

For this Algebra II project, students are divided into groups of three. One group member is responsible for bringing a box to school. From this box, the group members cut out a parabola from an equation. To do this, they create a coordinate plane on each side of the box. Using points from the upper two corners of the box and the origin, the students use the graphing calculator to find the quadratic regression. After drawing the parabola on the side of the box, they cut out the parabola and line the inside with a foil-wrapped poster board. They then find the focus point where they put the wire for cooking their hot dogs or marshmallows in the sun! Following are the instructions to the students.

Figure 19.1   Parabolic Solar Cooker

Parabolic Solar Cooker

1. Take your box and on the side find the exact center 1 inch from the bottom. This is your origin.

2. Create a coordinate plane with 1-inch intervals on the *x*- and *y*-axis (be as accurate as possible).

3. Determine the coordinates of the upper corners of your box. The two points are

   _____

   _____

4. Using these two points and the point (0, 0), use your calculator to come up with quadratic regression. The equation for your parabola is

   _____

   _____

5. Put the equation into your calculator and use the table feature to come up with several more points to graph. The points you used were

   _____

   _____

   _____

   _____

(Continued)

Figure 19.1 (Continued)

6. Plot these points and cut the parabola out of the box (again, as accurately as possible). Use the parabola you cut out to trace the other side of the box and cut that side out.

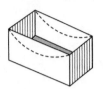

7. Cut a sheet of poster board that will fit exactly on the curve of the box, and then cover the sheet with foil.

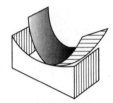

8. Tape down your poster board so it is secured to the box (to keep the foil from wrinkling).

9. Next, using your equation from Step 4, determine where your focus would be (show your work). The coordinates of your focus are

_____

_____

_____

_____

10. Using the scraps from your box, create a stand on each side of the box and mark where the focus should be. Cut a hole and insert the wire through. It should now be ready to test.

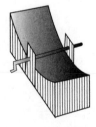

Note

1. Adapted with permission from *Principles and Standards for School Mathematics,* copyright © 2000 by the National Council of Teachers of Mathematics. All rights reserved.

▧ 20. Pascal's Triangle With Sequences and Series

Ken Petersen
Mountain View, Wyoming

Recommended Level: Grades 10–12

Overall Objective: Students will discover different sequences and series using Pascal's triangle (rows, row sums, diagonals, and diagonal sums).

Standards Met (Wyoming):

Number Operations and Concepts: Students represent and apply numbers in a variety of forms; apply the structures and properties of the real number system; explain their choice of estimation and problem solving strategies and justify results of solutions in problem-solving situations involving real numbers; use proportional reasoning to solve problems.

Geometry: Students communicate, using mathematical language to interpret, represent, or create geometric figures; draw or build figures from a mathematical description; analyze properties and determine attributes of two-dimensional objects. Students communicate the reasoning used in identifying geometric relationships in problem-solving situations; connect geometry with other mathematical topics.

Algebra: Students write, model, and evaluate expressions, functions, equations, and inequalities; connect algebra with other mathematical topics.

Data Analysis and Probability: Students determine, collect, organize, and analyze relevant data needed to make conclusions.

This lesson is primarily for pre-calculus students who have experience with sequences and series. In my class, they have used Pascal's triangle in previous lessons, so this is not their first time seeing it. I don't think, however, that a class needs to have seen Pascal's triangle before to do this lesson. I think that a simple explanation of how the triangle was created would be sufficient.

Figure 20.1 shows the handout for students with all of the questions for the lesson. The first question of the handout asks for the row explicit formula. Students need to add up the numbers in each of the rows and find an explicit formula that models their numbers. For illustration purposes, I have included a table to show the sums.

Row Number	1	2	3	4	5	6	n
Row Sum	1	2	4	8	16	32	?

Figure 20.1   Pascal's Triangle with Sequences and Series

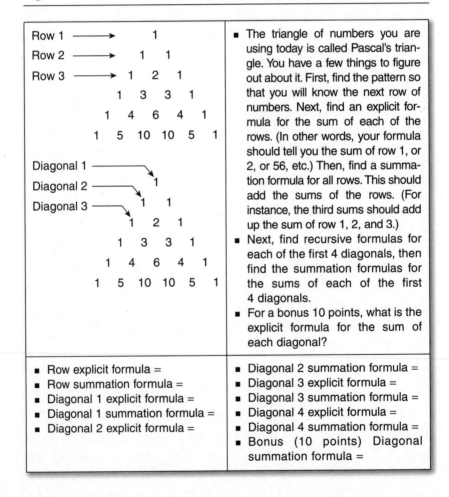

- Row explicit formula =
- Row summation formula =
- Diagonal 1 explicit formula =
- Diagonal 1 summation formula =
- Diagonal 2 explicit formula =

The triangle of numbers you are using today is called Pascal's triangle. You have a few things to figure out about it. First, find the pattern so that you will know the next row of numbers. Next, find an explicit formula for the sum of each of the rows. (In other words, your formula should tell you the sum of row 1, or 2, or 56, etc.) Then, find a summation formula for all rows. This should add the sums of the rows. (For instance, the third sums should add up the sum of row 1, 2, and 3.)

- Next, find recursive formulas for each of the first 4 diagonals, then find the summation formulas for the sums of each of the first 4 diagonals.
- For a bonus 10 points, what is the explicit formula for the sum of each diagonal?

- Diagonal 2 summation formula =
- Diagonal 3 explicit formula =
- Diagonal 3 summation formula =
- Diagonal 4 explicit formula =
- Diagonal 4 summation formula =
- Bonus (10 points) Diagonal summation formula =

Students immediately recognize this sequence of numbers as geometric, one that multiplies the previous term by a constant ratio. The common ratio is 2 and the explicit formula is 2^{n-1}. I encourage the students to type their formula into a graphing calculator and use the table to verify their results.

The next question asks students to recognize the pattern of the sum of each of the rows. This might be a little confusing at first. It asks the students to find the sum of row 1, then row 1 + row 2, then row 1 + row 2 + row 3, and so on. Below is a table that contains the sums.

Row Number	1	2	3	4	5	6	n
S_n	1	3	7	15	31	63	?

This summation typically gets students thinking a lot harder. Here is my suggestion if they can't figure it out. Have them add 1 to each of the sums. Now the numbers are 2, 4, 8, 16 . . . and they once again realize that they have a geometric sequence of numbers with an explicit formula of $2n - 1$ (quite similar to the other formula). Again, they should use a graphing calculator to check their results.

For the diagonals, I ask the students to find both the explicit formula and the summation formula. Diagonal 1 is illustrated as 1, 1, 1, 1 . . . and is quite easy to see that the explicit formula is 1. When students add the 1s together, they start to notice something interesting.

Row Number	1	2	3	4	5	6	n
Diagonal Sum	1	2	3	4	5	6	?

The sums of each of the 1's from diagonal 1 are the exact same sequence of numbers as diagonal 2. Therefore, the diagonal 1 summation formula is the diagonal 2 explicit formula. This applies to other diagonals as well.

One of the incredible things about Pascal's triangle is that the triangular numbers are contained in diagonal 3, the Fibonacci numbers can be found in the diagonals, square numbers can be made, and the list goes on and on.

There is a time, however, when it becomes difficult for students to recognize the formulas. At that point, I encourage them to use a TI-89 graphing calculator and use the summation feature to get the summation formula. After all, once they know the summation formula for a diagonal (D_n), they know the explicit formula for the next diagonal (D_{n+1}).

Last, I encourage students to find patterns with the explicit and summation formulas. Amazingly, students figure out a formula that correctly calculates the explicit or summation formula for *any* diagonal.

To end this lesson, I ask students to discover one more property about Pascal's triangle that they did not know existed and present it for the next class. I am still amazed by the power and the properties of this triangle.

21. Water Rocket Lesson

Ken Petersen
Mountain View, Wyoming

Recommended Level: Grades 10–12

Overall Objective: Students will learn the properties of parabolas, use trigonometry, and evaluate correlation coefficients for the accuracy of their water rocket launch models.

Standards Met (Wyoming):

Number Operations and Concepts: Students represent and apply numbers in a variety of forms; apply the structures and properties of the real number system; explain their choice of estimation and problem solving strategies and justify results of solutions in problem-solving situations involving real numbers; use proportional reasoning to solve problems.

Geometry: Students communicate, using mathematical language to interpret, represent, or create geometric figures; draw or build figures from a mathematical description; analyze properties and determine attributes of two-dimensional objects. Students communicate the reasoning used in identifying geometric relationships in problem-solving situations; connect geometry with other mathematical topics.

Measurement: Students identify and apply scale, ratios, and proportions in solving measurement problems.

Algebra: Students use algebraic concepts, symbols, and skills to represent and solve real-world problems; connect algebra with other mathematical topics.

Data Analysis and Probability: Students draw reasonable inferences from statistical data and/or correlation/best fit line to predict outcomes; determine, collect, organize, and analyze relevant data needed to make conclusions.

Materials Needed:

- Water rocket launching stand
- Soda pop bottles
- Low-temperature glue guns
- Cardboard
- Hard plastic (to make fins for the rocket)

I do the rocket project with both pre-calculus and calculus classes. However, any class with experience in trigonometry and quadratic function could do this activity. Of the materials needed for the students to build their own rockets, I typically supply the cardboard and the glue gun, and the students are responsible for the rest.

In calculus, when we do the rocket launches, we use the position function $(s(t) = -\frac{1}{2}gt^2 + v_0t + s_0)$, derive it to find the velocity function $(v(t) = -gt + v_0)$, and set the velocity function equal to zero. We do this because we know that the rocket is not moving at its highest point. Next, we solve for time. Once we know the time, we plug it back into the position function, and we've found a maximum on our graph, or the rocket's highest point.

However, I have primarily focused this lesson for the pre-calculus/ Algebra 2 class, in which we use parabolas. To begin, the students video record the flight of their rocket. We station a person 25 feet away from the rocket stand at all times. This person acts as a vertex of one of the many triangles the students will use to calculate the height. Once everyone has completed launching their rockets, the video is made available to them on computers. (When filming, I do not film up. I film side to side. It is imperative to have the 25-foot person on the screen while the rocket is going up so that students can measure the triangles on the rocket's flight upward. I do not have them do any measurements once it leaves the screen or while it is on its way down. It is imperative, though, that the rocket's landing is filmed for total elapsed flight time.)

Students use protractors to measure the rocket's angle of elevation. They find the horizontal line that connects the person who marks 25 feet from the stand and the top of their rocket. The last frame that the rocket is on the stand will be their first point (0,0). This represents zero time and zero height (see Figure 21.1).

Figure 21.1   First Calculation

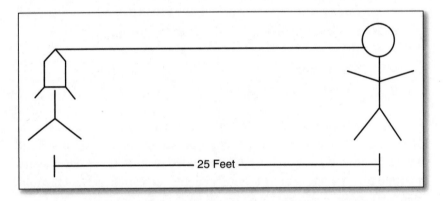

25 Feet

The next step is to advance the video one frame. They notice the rocket has started its flight, and they use the tip of the rocket to form a triangle (see Figure 21.2). Now the students have two choices to find the rocket's height. First, they can use right triangle trigonometry. The height of the rocket is the length of angle θ's opposite side. The side they know is angle θ's adjacent side. Since the tangent function relates opposite to adjacent, students use

$$\tan \theta = \frac{height}{25\ feet}.$$

Simplifying, students come up with $25\tan \theta = height$. Once they've calculated the height, they note the corresponding time (measured in thirtieths of a second). This process continues until the rocket has completely left the screen.

Figure 21.2   Second Calculation

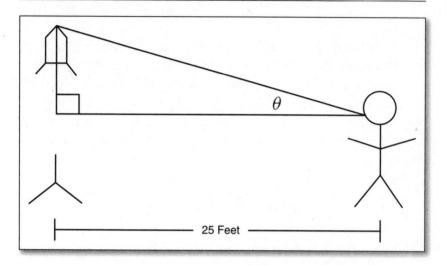

The second choice students have is to use the Law of Sines:

$$\frac{\sin A}{a} = \frac{\sin B}{b} = \frac{\sin C}{c}.$$

To use this law, students must know an angle and a side opposite. They know the top angle of the triangle (next to the rocket) by using their knowledge of triangles. Every triangle has 180 degrees. They know it is a right triangle because the rocket travels vertically, and they made a horizontal line that connects the 25-foot person with the rocket stand. Next, they measured angle θ; now they can calculate the top angle of the triangle. The side opposite of the top angle is 25 feet. The next step with the Law of Sines is to find another angle and side of the triangle. They could use the 90-degree angle, but they quickly learn that the distance from the person to the flying rocket is irrelevant. Therefore, they use the angle by the person marking the 25 feet. The opposite side of this angle is the height of their rocket. Using the earlier illustration, here is how a student might use the Law of Sines:

$$\frac{\sin(90 - \theta)}{25} = \frac{\sin \theta}{height}.$$

Next, the students solve for the height, thus obtaining

$$height = \frac{25 \sin \theta}{\sin(90 - \theta)} \cdot$$

Once the rocket comes back on the screen, the students calculate the total elapsed time for the rocket to hit the ground. This gives them their final time and height ordered pair to find their quadratic equation.

Students enter the times and heights they calculated from the rocket flight into a calculator and have it compute a quadratic regression. This regression is in the form $y = ax^2 + bx + c$. Students first use the quadratic formula

$$\left(\frac{-b \pm \sqrt{b^2 - 4ac}}{2a} \right)$$

to calculate the x intercepts. These should be very close to the two times their rockets were on the ground (takeoff and landing). Next, they find the line of symmetry by averaging the two x intercepts, or by simplifying $\frac{-b}{2a}$. Last, they plug the line of symmetry into the quadratic equation and the resulting number is the vertex or, more interestingly, the rocket's maximum height.

The final step I ask the students to complete is to use Geometer's Sketchpad to plot the x intercepts, line of symmetry, and vertex they discovered. They use the graph feature and plot the quadratic equation. Students love the reinforcement of seeing they did everything correctly. (This is an optional step, but the majority of students do it.)

Helpful Tips

- There are a few things I encourage the students to be critical about during this project. I don't give them these answers, but here are a few that I would consider. One is that they never find times and heights of the rocket coming down, only when it hits the ground. My primary reason for this is that the resulting x intercepts will be extremely close to the times the rocket is on the ground. Students make better connections with the project and the math with this modification. If a student's rocket is in the air for seven seconds, they will notice that one of their x intercepts is seven. When they discover the other x intercept is zero, they make the connection about what these two numbers really represent.

- I used to have the students find all heights and times, but I noticed unnecessary student confusion because the rocket's time was not accurately modeled by the quadratic equation they found. This was due to wind resistance, lost rocket parts during flight, and slower times when the rocket was coming down. By using the times and heights as I previously mentioned, the quadratic equations students create have near 100% accuracy, thus providing a clear connection between the rocket path and the quadratic equation.
- Students are able to make amazing discoveries with this project. It is also great to see their competitive natures come to life during the whole process of the project. They talk friendly "trash" with each other, and they have an enormous amount of pride in their creations. The trash talk even extends to me because I am part of this competition every year. I would encourage you to be a part, as well, and make special competition rules if their rocket(s) can beat yours.
- Through the years, I've made several modifications to this project. Some have been from student evaluations, and some have been from me. Regardless, the rocket project is great for the students because they are able to create their own flying machine. It's great for me because they enhance their knowledge of parabolas in standard form, trigonometry, triangle properties, and correlation coefficients; but most important, they get a love for higher-level math.

PART III

Teaching Language Arts and Social Studies

Teaching Language Arts

Overview, Chapters 22–29

22. **Judy Osburn Beemer,** a literacy coach in Junction City, Kansas, demonstrates an easy-to-remember method to help students recognize subordinate conjunctions and learn related comma usage. She presents the lesson in the context of a writing workshop that also promotes sentence fluency and variety—the trait that has the most impact on writing scores.

23. **Alicia Deel,** a special education teacher in Grundy, Virginia, shows how having students redesign a restaurant menu can improve their descriptive and technical writing skills using adjectives.

24. **Rebecca Snyder**, a language arts teacher from Latrobe, Pennsylvania, has students reconstruct models of professional and student writing to perceive the purpose behind the techniques effective writers routinely employ. By deconstructing the writing process at the sentence level, students concentrate more closely on the revision of their own writing to improve focus, organization, content, clarity, and style.

25. **Alicia Deel,** in a second lesson, creates a *story stew,* a visual activity that introduces students to the concepts of character, plot, and setting in a story.

26. **Rebecca Snyder** presents a second lesson in which students design their own study guides by choosing before-, during-, and after-reading activities from a menu of *appetizers, entrees,* and *desserts.* Menu items target multiple learning styles, as well as students' varied interests and

abilities, helping teachers differentiate reading activities for a broad and diverse range of students.

27. **Jill Pinard,** an English teacher in Weare, New Hampshire, groups students in pairs to prepare a dramatic reading and narrative pantomime based on a selection from Edgar Lee Masters' *Spoon River Anthology.*

28. **Spencer Arnaud,** an English teacher from Arnaudsville, Louisiana, uses a modified debate approach to have students argue positions and support their opinions on current topics. The students acquire skills that are needed to access information resources through library research and synthesis of supporting evidence.

29. **Elizabeth G. Lutz-Hackett,** an English teacher in Yellow Springs, Ohio, uses Ernest Hemingway's "A Clean Well Lighted Place" to guide students in exploring the imagery of light and dark, the characterization of the young and old waiters, and the application of Erik Erikson's theory of development.

22. Take Me Out to the Ball Game: Building Sentence Sense Without Teaching Grammar

Judy Osburn Beemer
Junction City, Kansas

Recommended Level: Grades 7–12

Overall Objective: Students will distinguish complete sentences from fragments and correctly place commas after clauses beginning with subordinate conjunctions. Students will learn the importance and sound of sentence variety in writing.

Standards Met (Kansas):

Writing: Uses a variety of sentence structures and lengths; creates a variety of sentence beginnings that relate to and build upon previous sentences but move the reader easily through the text; uses fragments only for stylistic effect; uses correct mechanics and punctuation to guide the reader through the text; uses the comma, which may be manipulated for stylistic effect and may contribute to clarity.

Reading: Reads fluently.

Materials Needed:

- Current reading materials, class or independent
- Index cards
- Timer
- Candy or gum or other prizes
- Magic slates: white paper inserted into plastic page protectors to create miniature whiteboards
- Dry-erase markers and tissues for erasers
- Old drinking glass
- Thick towel
- Hammer

Over many years of teaching and literacy coaching, I often heard the same repeated comments from English teachers:

- Sentence fluency? These kids don't even know what a sentence is!
- I'm so tired of kids answering questions in fragments!
- Why do grade-school teachers tell kids they can't ever start a sentence with *because?*
- I went through school during the whole-language movement. I don't know how to teach punctuation. I don't even know the rules myself!

I understood their frustrations. Whenever I tried to explain the reasons for common punctuation, I found that my students knew too little grammar to apply the rules. I didn't want to stop to teach pure grammar lessons when my true goal was to improve their writing. After I heard Jeff Anderson (2005) present ideas for incorporating grammar, usage, and style instruction into writers' workshops, I decided to follow his lead and develop a sample lesson that gave students clear reasons for placing commas without teaching grammar per se. Part I: Take Me Out to the Ballgame, is the result.

More than just teaching comma placement, though, I wanted to develop students' *sentence sense.* All too well, I remembered late-night essay grading, when my head nodded over sentence after sentence that marched monotonously to the same beat, without variety or pacing related to meaning. Even if students could plant commas in the right places, they needed to do much more. They needed an awareness of the rhythm of written and spoken language. They needed practice in creating that rhythm. They needed to *feel* the suspense of a periodic sentence, the "measure heaped upon measure" effect of multiple compound sentences. Part II: Mix It Up, Baby, is a beginning step toward developing that sentence sense.

Part I: Take Me Out to the Ball Game

Say the following to your students: "I have discovered that students don't always recognize what makes a sentence. So in an effort to increase your sentence sense, we're going to play around with a certain group of words and look at what they do to sentences. Here's a goofy way to remember these words: AAAWW-WUBBIS. (Say it long, drawn-out, like a cheer) Repeat after me . . . AAAWW-WUBBIS!" Each letter stands for a word:

A = although (and though and even though)	W = where (and wherever)
A = as (and as long as and as soon as)	U = until
	B = before
A = after	B = because
W = when (and whenever)	I = if
W = while	S = since

Have students practice remembering the word each initial letter stands for; then ask the following:

1. What's the term for a word formed by combining the initial letters of other words? *(acronym)*

2. What are the word parts in *acronym?* (*acro* or *acros* and *nym*)

3. What do they mean? (Encourage students to think of other words that use those same word parts [*acrobat; acropolis*—city at the top of a hill; *pseudonym*] and to intuit a meaning. [*acro* = at the top or end; *nym* = name].)

4. How does *acronym* fit these meanings?

5. Is AAAWW-WUBBIS a true acronym? (No. It is only a coined word, not a real one.)

"To help you remember the words, we're going to have an AAAWW-WUBBIS scavenger hunt. The girls are the AAAWW team, and the boys are the WUBBIS team. Say it for me. (Point to the girls, who say "AAAWW," and point to the guys, who say "WUBBIS!") Work individually to find and copy, depending on your team, either AAAWW- or WUBBIS-starting sentences in (name whatever story the class is currently reading). Each sentence goes onto a separate note card. Whichever group finds and copies the most sentences wins. Can I explain anything again or better? You have four minutes. Go!" (Walk around to help individual students and to answer questions. After four minutes, call time and determine which team wins. Give them candy, gum, or another prize).

Activity 1: Sift and sort. Now, mixing the team members, divide students into triads, each person bringing along his or her note cards. The task this time is to determine what questions AAAWW-WUBBIS sentence parts answer. They should sort their collective note cards into piles in which the AAAWW-WUBBIS-part answers the same question, and then list the questions on their slates.

Activity 2: What do you see? Next, group by shoulder partners. Each pair should answer the following question: "What do you notice about sentences that start with an AAAWW-WUBBIS part? How are they alike? Write your answer on your magic slate" (see materials list). (Answers could be: The sentences are always in two parts, the sentences always have a comma.) Ask "Why?" and discuss their theories.

Activity 3: Make a metaphor. Ask them to think of something they could compare AAAWW-WUBBIS-starting sentences to, something that happens in two parts (wind-up and pitch, for example). Have them write their answers as a metaphor on their slates: "AAAWW-WUBBIS-starting sentences are windups and pitches." Share responses. Call attention to what their voices do at the end of the AAAWW-WUBBIS part and at the end of the entire sentence. Ask what it means when we let our voices go up at the end of a sentence part. What feeling do our voices convey? (A sense of anticipation, incompleteness, more to follow.)

Activity 4: Make an inference. "Is an AAAWW-WUBBIS part by itself a complete sentence? Why not? Do think-write-pair-share. Discuss."

Activity 5: Play umpire. First, draw on another metaphor: What's the difference between a ball and a strike in baseball? Which one is the "real thing" (a strike)? A ball is a wannabe strike, but not the real thing. Is an AAAWW-WUBBIS part a ball or a strike? Explain, or better yet, have students explain.

Divide into the original AAAWW-WUBBIS teams. Have a student from one team read either a complete sentence or just the AAAWW-WUBBIS part. Students on the other team write "ball" or "strike" on their slates to indicate if they heard a fragment or a complete sentence, then show them to you on the count of three. You can easily determine which students understand. Then switch roles on the teams. Continue until most slates show correct responses.

Activity 6: Fragments. Now add another metaphor. Be dramatic: Cover an old glass with several towels and strike its edge with a hammer, just enough to chip away a piece of the rim. Ask students what they might call one of the pieces. Lead them to the term *fragment,* and ask them how that word is an appropriate metaphor for an AAAWW-WUBBIS-part. Show how the fragment cannot be drunk from by itself but, rather, has to be "glued" to the remaining glass. In the same way, an AAAWW-WUBBIS part must be glued to the sentence; it cannot make a sentence all by itself.

Activity 7: Free write (perhaps a homework assignment). Tell them, "As individuals, your next job is to write an acrostic poem. Can you figure out from the word parts in *acrostic* what an acrostic poem might be?" (*acros* = at the tip or end; in an acrostic poem, the writer uses the "tip-letter" or initial of a word to write a line of poetry.) "You should write AAAWW-WUBBIS vertically, one letter on every other line. Using the word the first letter stands for, write a complete sentence that begins with the AAAWW-WUBBIS-part. Be sure to punctuate correctly. Then, move down to the next letter and write an AAAWW-WUBBIS-part sentence for it that relates in content to your first sentence. Keep going through all the letters. You'll end up with a ten-sentence story written in poetry form, each line starting with a different AAAWW-WUBBIS-word." (You may need to model.)

Part II: Mix It Up, Baby

Activity 1: Recognize voice and sentence pattern. During the next day's class, have students volunteer to share their AAAWW-WUBBIS acrostic poems. Pick one that is especially monotonous in voice and sentence length, and say, "This assignment was good for practicing AAAWW-WUBBIS parts, but it was not so good for producing fluent writing. Listen." Read that poem, and draw the length and voice pattern of each sentence on the board (Payne, 1982) to show how it repeats, like a stuck CD:

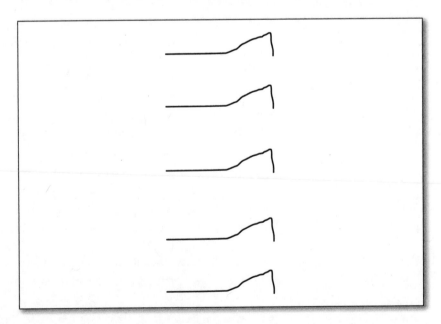

Ask, "Do you like the sound of the same voice and sentence pattern repeated like that?" (They'll probably say no, that it's boring.)

Activity 2: Mix it up. Either project the sample acrostic or hand out copies, and ask how the students can vary the sentence patterns to fit the meaning and make the story flow. Model and revise together. (You may want to distribute lists of transitional/text-structure words to help students pull the sentences together and show the relationships between them.)

When finished, draw sentence line graphs to represent the different patterns and lengths:

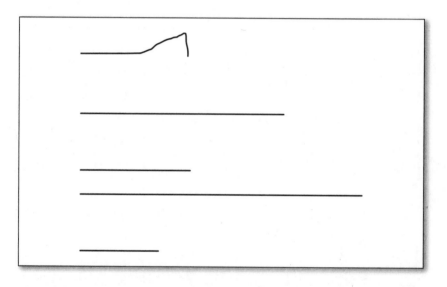

Activity 3: Listen to the rhythm. Read a passage from whatever literature you're studying that illustrates varied sentence length and pattern. Have students use their slates to diagram the voice and sentence lengths and patterns. Discuss the effect of both a short sentence in the midst of several long ones (emphasis) and a series of sentences that intentionally follow the same pattern (parallel structure). Have them listen for the rhythms.

Activity 4: Assign. Tell students, "Take your acrostic and revise it to make a fluent story, with varied sentence lengths and patterns that fit the meaning. Mix it up, baby!" Then, share the new versions of the stories and celebrate.

Helpful Tips

- The activities provided are easily adapted across the curriculum. A teacher could boost reading as well as expository writing skills through the recognition of AAAWW-WUBBIS words in text from various subject areas.
  - AAAWW-WUBBIS is similar to "if, then" statements in science and research and could be used to set up inquiry lessons.
  - In social studies, AAAWW-WUBBIS sets up the cause and effect situation.
  - Students could use this to write their own word problems in math classes.
  - For current events, students could create sentences to answer the *why, when, where,* and *how* questions with AAAWW-WUBBIS.
  - AAAWW-WUBBIS could easily shift into the reading classroom to help students comprehend complex sentences.
  - Advanced students could compare the use of AAAWW-WUBBIS words in a novel and in a science text, as a style analysis.
  - For younger students, the teacher might provide text for analysis with modeling on how to recognize AAAWW-WUBBIS words and their effects.
- Classroom displays of AAAWW-WUBBIS poems could keep the concept in the forefront of students' minds all year.
- Hands-on adaptation: Create flash cards with different parts of the sentence and different punctuation marks. Then have students find the correct matches to make a sentence.

References

Anderson, J. (2005). *Mechanically inclined: Building grammar, usage and style into writer's workshop.* Portland, ME: Stenhouse.

Payne, L. V. (1982). *The Lively Art of Writing.* River Grove, IL: Follett.

℞   23. Descriptive Diner

Alicia Deel
Grundy, Virginia

Recommended Level: Grades 9–12

Overall Objective: The students will be able to identify descriptive words (adjectives) and effectively use descriptive words in writing.

Standards Met (Virginia): The student will develop narrative, literary, expository, and technical writings to inform, explain, analyze, or entertain; Develop a variety of writings with an emphasis on exposition; Write in a variety of forms with an emphasis on persuasion; Develop expository and technical writings.

Materials Needed:

- Restaurant menus (Visual examples are very helpful when working with students with special needs.)
- Dictionaries
- Thesauruses
- Construction paper, glue, and pencils, or a computer with a design program (Microsoft Publisher)

I created this activity to help students develop a more descriptive vocabulary while gaining an understanding of adjectives and their purpose in writing. The students redesign a restaurant menu to make the food items sound more appetizing by adding descriptive words (adjectives).

Activity

1. Give students a restaurant menu (it can be an actual menu from a restaurant or one that was created).

2. Have the students brainstorm words that will describe the food items (examples: *tasty, delicious*).

3. Have the students write a short description of food items using the adjectives they came up with during the brainstorming session.

4. Have the students illustrate and design their menus on construction paper or a computer if one is available.

Helpful Tips

This activity works well in an inclusion classroom. The students can be divided into groups. The teacher can instruct each group to design and develop a menu. The teacher may want to choose a peer tutor for each group if working in an inclusion classroom.

---

24. Deconstructing the Writer's Craft

Rebecca Snyder
Latrobe, Pennsylvania

Recommended Level: Grades 10–12

Overall Objective: Students will be able to identify and imitate the structural techniques and stylistic devices an author uses to increase focus, organization, coherence, and clarity of expository text.

Standards Met: Write using well-developed content appropriate for the topic; write fully developed paragraphs that have details and information specific to the topic and relevant to the focus. Write with controlled and/or subtle organization; sustain a logical order throughout the piece. Write with a command of the stylistic aspects of composition; use different types and lengths of sentences; use precise language. Revise writing to improve style, word choice, sentence variety, and subtlety of meaning after rethinking how questions of purpose, audience, and genre have been addressed.

Materials Needed:

- Professional essay excerpt, one to two paragraphs in length
- Individual student writing samples, one to two paragraphs in length
- Scissors*
- Multicolored highlighters*
- Overhead projector*

*These items are only necessary if students are unable to manipulate electronic versions of the samples and an interactive whiteboard is not available.

I type each sentence of a paragraph or two from a professional essay model separately (print and cut into strips if using hard copies). I choose the professional exemplar according to which devices or techniques my student-writers are struggling to master. I have found that a good model for this lesson will provide effective and explicit coherence devices, transitions, and rhetorical devices. The topic can be connected to current classroom content or student interests. Whatever the topic, the most important criteria for model selection is how effectively it utilizes the element(s) of writing that I am attempting to target with my students. I have found that this lesson works particularly well for teaching transitions, organization, and sentence length.

Part 1: Reassembling the Model Paragraph

Assign students to small cooperative groups. Ask them to assemble the sentence strips (either electronically or using print copies) into an order they think is coherent and may best approximate the original. If they have difficulty getting started, first model the process by engaging in a "think aloud." I invite students to listen and watch as I take a moment to walk through the process I would use to determine a possible organization for the paragraph. I go so far as to identify the topic or introductory sentence and then isolate two strips as possible choices for what comes next.

After constructing their own version of the paragraph, I encourage the groups to have the designated reporter read the finished product to the rest of the group. Then, I ask students to explain why they arranged the sentences as they did. Is the paragraph coherent? What is the main idea? What helped you to decide which ideas to put first and which to use for conclusion?

Discussion that follows usually spotlights the words, phrases, and devices that the writer employs to introduce, connect, and elaborate upon his or her ideas. An extension of the discussion begins to pinpoint the author's use of stylistic devices. Aiding their ability to assemble the paragraph coherently, students usually cite repeated or related words and phrases, ideas that range from the broad to the specific, as well as transitional words and phrases.

As each group shares with the class, I record their observations and ideas, as well as a list of the cited words and phrases from the paragraph in a central location—either an interactive whiteboard or a transparency. Students could also be asked to sort and then color-code by device or technique the components of the paragraph mentioned in discussion.

The original paragraph, if not replicated fully by one of the groups, is finally revealed. I sometimes invite students to reflect in writing or again in discussion on how their version differed. Higher-level writers may also be encouraged at this point to justify the author's organization and stylistic choices.

Part 2: Comparing Models

Ask students to employ the same process with a student-generated paragraph from a previous year. If this model is chosen carefully, students add to the list generated in the preceding discussion or begin to pull items from that list that would improve their ability to reconstruct this student model.

Discussion after this section of the activity should encourage students to evaluate which paragraph they were able to assemble more readily—the professional or student model.

- What made one paragraph easier to reconstruct than the other?
- What did the writer do that helped you, the reader?
- How can we mirror these moves in our own writing?
- What could you use from this list of elements to revise the student model?

Part 3: Examining Their Own Writing

Students now apply the same process with a partner using pieces of their own writing. I usually ask students to choose an excerpt from an essay they have already handed in. Students could also use a current draft of an assignment they are struggling to revise. After typing and separating each sentence, student partners exchange print copies of their strips or electronic copies via a shared drive or e-mail. Each student thinks through a reconstruction of his or her partner's original.

Both students then share their compositions while discussing the difficulties encountered and the elements that proved helpful in attempting to rebuild the paragraph.

Finally, I ask students to complete a written reflection on the exercise. For homework, students are asked to complete a revision of their paragraph that they examined with a partner.

HelpfulTips

- The first part of the activity could be used as a reading activity to explore a stated and/or implied main idea.
- If you are using hard copies of the sentences, you could save instructional time by cutting the first two models into strips before the lesson.
- When students are using hard copies of their own writing, retyping the sentences with enough space between them to cut a clean line helps them to avoid ending up with a set of puzzle pieces. Students should use the text, not the shape of the cutting, to determine the placement of the sentences.
- The professional model could come from an essay the students either have studied in class or will study in class. Students may engage in "reading as writers" more readily after examining course texts as examples of good writing.
- Students could be asked to arrange their sentence strips individually first and then come to consensus in the small group on the order of the sentences.
- To provide an additional challenge, do not reveal the topic of the paragraph, and ask students to articulate its main idea once they have completed the reconstruction.
- Students who are struggling with content development could be asked to color-code and highlight their sentence strips (for electronic copies this can be done using the highlighting

(Continued)

(Continued)

tool in Microsoft Word) according to these three categories: main idea (topic sentence or point), supporting details (illustrations or evidence), and concluding statement or transition. Students who often omit supporting details or do not provide enough of them now have a visual indicator of the missing content.

- Students could be given the original arrangement of a second professional essay and then be asked to provide an effective alternative arrangement. Discussion could focus on how writers make decisions concerning organization.

25. Story Stew

Alicia Deel
Grundy, Virginia

Recommended Level: Grades 9–12

Overall Objective: Students will be able to recognize character traits and relationships among characters, the plot of the story and how it is developed, the setting of the story (where it is located), and the mood of the story.

Standards Met (Virginia): The student will apply knowledge of the characteristics and elements of various literary forms; Make planned oral presentations; Participate in and report small-group learning activities.

Materials Needed:

- Apron
- Large cooking pot
- Wooden spoon
- Story
- 5 × 7 inch index cards, which will act as recipe cards (Multi-colored index cards work best. Choose one color for characters, one color for plot, and one color for setting.)

This lesson plan (modified from www.teacher.net) provides a visual introduction to the elements of literature—the concepts of characters, setting, and plot of a story.

Activity

1. Put on an apron, and set a cooking pot and spoon on your desk. Tell the students that they are going to make story stew. Explain that a good story is like stew—it has a lot of ingredients.

2. Reach into the pot and pull out an index card on which is written the word *characters*. Explain to the students that characters are those whom the story is about. Mention familiar stories, and ask students who the characters are in each story.

3. Reach into the pot and pull out another index card on which the word *setting* is written. Explain to the students that the setting is where and when the story happens or takes place. Mention familiar stories, and ask students to identify the setting in each.

4. Reach into the pot again and pull out a final index card on which is written the word *plot*. Explain that plot is what happens in a story. Talk about familiar stories, and ask students to briefly explain the plot in each.

5. After this introduction of characters, setting, and plot, read a short story to the students. (You should choose a story with few characters, a well-defined setting, and a simple plot.)

6. Ask the students to identify the characters in the story and write them on an index card. Have them drop the index card into the cooking pot, and you stir up the stew.

7. Ask the students to identify the setting and the plot in the same way.

8. After stirring up the ingredients, reach into the pot and produce a picture of the story that you just read to the students.

Helpful Tips

- You can ask students to create their own Story Stew by having them make up their own characters, setting, and a simple plot description and write them on index cards. Then have them develop a story using their own elements.
- For students with special needs in an inclusion classroom, provide index cards with story elements (characters, setting, plot) written on them, and let students choose one from each element to write a story about.
- This activity could also be completed in groups, especially in an inclusion classroom with peer tutors. Each group could develop and make an oral presentation of their story.

26. Catering to Student Needs: Menu-Style Study Guides

Rebecca Snyder
Latrobe, Pennsylvania

Recommended Level: Grades 7–12

Overall Objective: Students will be able to choose and employ effective reading strategies during all phases of the reading process in order to aid their comprehension and interpretation of a novel.

Standards Met: Demonstrate after-reading understanding and interpretation of both fiction and nonfiction text, including public documents; Identify, describe, evaluate, and synthesize the essential ideas in text; Assess those reading strategies that were most effective in learning from a variety of texts; Read and respond to nonfiction and fiction, including poetry and drama; read and understand works of literature.

Materials Needed:

- Prepared menu of activities
- Publishing software for the creation of menu pages

- Binders or three-clasp folders (portfolios)

In order to engage students in the reading process during a novel study, I ask students to determine which strategies and activities will work best for them through the creation of an independent study guide from what I refer to as a menu of appetizers, entrees, and desserts. Students choose a variety of activities and even create a few of their own, requiring them to consider carefully which strategies they find useful and interesting, which activities are the best medium for digesting portions of the text, and which projects would allow for expression of their individual connections to the novel. Instead of relying on teacher-generated materials, students take an active role in connecting with the text before, during, and after reading.

I first create a list of activities or projects that target a wide range of learning styles, appeal to multiple interests, and require thinking skills at all levels of Bloom's (1956) taxonomy. I chart these activities in tiers according to the skill level each activity targets and the stage of the reading process in which the activity should be completed (see Figure 26.1 for the teacher's planner). For instance, gathering information about the time period in which the novel is set may be a first-tier, before-reading activity (appetizer). Creating a wiki page that charts character relationships could appear as a second-tier, during-reading activity (entree).

I then use the planner to compose an actual restaurant menu for an establishment whose name incorporates the novel theme or title. The menu is created with publishing software in order to make it both visually appealing and easy to follow. Each set of activities (appetizers, entrees, desserts) is given its own page in a three-ring binder or folder (portfolio). Clip art, pictures, and creative fonts are used to style the menu pages according to the novel's setting, themes, or characters. Each student receives his or her own menu.

Students are required to "taste" items during each "course" of the meal, or novel unit. They must choose a predetermined number of appetizers and create and complete at least one of their own to add to the menu. These before-reading activities can serve as an anticipation

Figure 26.1   Menu Study Guide Planner (for use by the teacher)

Tiers	First Course Appetizers	Second Course Entrees	Third Course Desserts
TIER 1 ACTIVITIES "Lighter Fare"			
TIER 2 ACTIVITIES "House Specialties"			
TIER 3 ACTIVITIES "Hearty Helpings" or "Made to Share"			

guide, include stance questions, or ask students to begin making personal connections to the characters, themes, or events of the novel.

During reading, I ask students to choose from entrees that require them to engage actively in the reading of the text. A variety of activities are available to students in the dessert section of the menu as well. The after-reading activities provide summative assessment and enrichment opportunities.

Reader's theater presentations, role-plays, and multimedia projects, along with paper and pencil tasks, throughout the menu help me to cater to individual student abilities, learning styles, and interests. Student-created menu items in each section provide opportunities for students to explore elements of the novel that they find particularly interesting while deepening their level of engagement in independent reading.

I ask students to choose a variety of menu items from each of the sections. First-tier activities are "Lighter Fare." Second-tier options are "House Specialties," and third tier items are "Hearty Helpings." Sometimes, I even add a "Made-to-Share" section that includes opportunities for cooperative learning and reflection with a partner or small group.

Students use the menu (folder or binder) to organize their completed activities, reflections, assessments, and so on. At the completion of the novel study, students have a portfolio that serves as a way to assess their learning and participation in the unit.

Helpful Tips

- One way to gain more control over the level of activities students choose is to create a "medical alert card" for each student that lists his or her "dietary restrictions."
- Menu items can be titled creatively, making connections between the activities, actual recipes, and elements of the novel, such as "Jay Gatsby's Speakeasy Soup" or "Wiki-Watermelon Slices."
- The menu can be adapted for literature circles. Student groups can create the titles for menu items based on the book they are reading and choose "plates" either as a group or individually.

Reference

Bloom, B. S. (1956). *Taxonomy of educational objectives, Handbook I: The cognitive domain.* New York: David McKay.

◪ 27. Navigating *Spoon River* While Putting Your Students in the Spotlight

Jill Pinard
Weare, New Hampshire

Recommended Level: Grades 11–12

Overall Objective: Students will practice close reading of a text by bringing a piece of literature to life audibly and physically.

Standards Met: Identify literary devices as appropriate to genre (e.g., similes, metaphors, alliteration, rhyme scheme, onomatopoeia, imagery, repetition, flashback, foreshadowing, personification, hyperbole, symbolism, allusion, diction, syntax, bias, or point of view); Examine characterization (e.g., stereotype, antagonist, protagonist), motivation, or interactions (including relationships), citing thoughts, words, or actions that reveal character traits, motivations, or changes over time; Use a variety of strategies of address (e.g., eye contact, speaking rate, volume, articulation, enunciation, pronunciation, inflection, voice modulation, intonation, rhythm, and gesture) to communicate ideas effectively.

Materials Needed:

- TV/DVD player or projector
- BessKepp, "Rotten Pomegranates," *Russell Simmons Presents Def Poetry: Season 4.* HBO Home Video, 2002 (or another example of contemporary performance poetry)
- Selections from Edgar Lee Masters' *Spoon River Anthology* or other poems that are dramatic monologues

I am always a little surprised when students enter my classes at the beginning of the year and ask with dread, "Do we have to do poetry this year?" Students generally like writing poetry, but they act as though reading it is more painful than having their braces tightened.

I try to diffuse my students' poetry angst by exposing them to a wide range of works frequently. This lesson engages students in a close reading of a poem that they will then perform for the class.

Act I: Introduction

- Show BessKepp performing his poem "Rotten Pomegranates." Conduct a whole-class discussion of how BessKepp uses his voice and body to help express the imagery and emotion of his poem. Point out how his stance, facial expressions, and gestures help convey the poem.
- Introduce Edgar Lee Masters' *Spoon River Anthology,* a collection of 244 epitaphs each written in the voice of one of inhabitants of the Spoon River cemetery.

Act II: Rehearsal

- Distribute the student handout (see Figure 27.1)
- In pairs, have students choose a selection from *Spoon River* to study and, ultimately, present.
- Have pairs work through their chosen texts, analyzing them for content and literary elements.
- Have pairs plan how to read and pantomime to help illustrate that character's story.
- Have pairs rehearse.

Act III: Performance and Reflection

- Final performances. Each pair performs for the class: one person recites (or reads) the chosen section, while the other person acts it out.
- Conduct a brief whole-class discussion after each presentation. Ask the class what they understood about each character. Ask the performers what they hoped we would understand about their character.
- As an extension for the whole class, read, perform, or watch Thornton Wilder's *Our Town.*

Figure 27.1 Navigating *Spoon River*

Spoon River Anthology, by Edgar Lee Masters, is a collection of 244 epitaphs written in the voice of inhabitants of the Spoon River cemetery. You and your classmates will be putting them on their feet.

Part I

Carefully read through your chosen epitaph a few times. This is poetry, so every word counts!

- What do we know about this person?
- Try reading it aloud to hear if you notice anything new.
- Think about the person's name.
- What appears to be his or her role in the town?
- Do we trust this person?

Part II

Now prepare for your performance. You and your partner need to decide who will be the speaker's voice and who will be his or her body; then, work together.

- How would this person speak? (loudly, quickly, slowly, confidently, quietly, nervously, etc.)
- Which words would he or she emphasize? Which words might he or she not want us to catch?
- How does this person walk into a room? Which part of his or her body do you notice first (face, hands, torso, etc.)?
- How can you use your body to help convey what he or she is saying? Try to avoid providing literal, physical translations of the words (try not to be a doo-wop back-up singer).

Evaluative Criteria

Effective verbal expression

Effective use of body

Focus

Imagination

Accurate representation of the character

Evidence of preparation

HelpfulTips

- While I cite specific texts for this lesson, this sequence would work with a variety of texts, including primary source documents, and can be modified for use in middle school or Grades 9 and 10.

- This lesson begins by using contemporary performance poetry as a hook or grabber. I find that while many students express discomfort with poetry, they are captivated by contemporary performance poetry. I love the Def Poetry series, which is widely available on DVD, but teachers must preview them carefully because many of the pieces are wildly inappropriate for school. "Money" by Poetri is another of my favorites from Def Poetry and is a great example of an extended metaphor.

- As students become more comfortable with poetry, they might become interested in participating in the Poetry Out Loud National Recitation Project that is sponsored by the National Endowment for the Arts and The Poetry Foundation (see www.poetryoutloud.org).

- This lesson could also serve as an effective introduction to a unit on public speaking. My students must present a memorized, formal speech every year so I try to provide numerous smaller opportunities to practice being alone in the front of the class. Performing a short poem in front of the class is a more comfortable first step.

- For more information on integrating dramatic arts into other disciplines, consult the following texts: Cornett, C. E. (2002). *Creating meaning through literature and the arts: An integration resource for classroom teachers.* Upper Saddle River, NJ: Prentice Hall PTR. Walker, P. P. (1993). *Bring in the arts: Improvisations in dramatics, art, and story writing for elementary and middle school classrooms.* Chicago: Heinemann.

28. "Let's Argue!" A Research-Oriented Approach to Classroom Debates

Spencer Arnaud
Arnaudsville, Louisiana

Recommended Level: Grades 10–12

Overall Objective: Given topics of current concern, students will prepare logical arguments to support one side of an issue. Students will support and defend arguments based on the identification, analysis, and synthesis of information resources.

Standards Met: Students will solve problems using reasoning skills, including using supporting evidence to verify solutions and analyzing relationships between prior knowledge, life experiences, and information in text; Develop organized, coherent paragraphs that include topic sentences, logical sequence, transitional words and phrases, and appropriate closing sentences; Deliver clear, coherent, and concise oral presentations and responses about information and ideas in a variety of texts; Participate in group and panel discussions; Locate, analyze, and synthesize information from grade-appropriate resources, including multiple printed texts, specialized dictionaries, periodicals, electronic sources, and community or government data.

Materials Needed:

- Internet access
- *Reader's Guide to Periodical Literature* access
- Library access (books, specialized dictionaries, periodicals)

In this lesson, students become familiar with debating techniques through informal classroom debates. They also develop the skills needed to effectively support their arguments through more formal debates. Through the course of their research, students become familiar with different information resources that can be used to find logical support for their arguments.

Activity 1: Selection of Debatable Topics

About a week before the lesson is to begin, explain to students that they will be debating issues of current concern. Each student is to read the newspaper, watch the evening news, and participate in discussions with parents in an effort to produce 10 topics that are of current concern and are debatable. Explain that *debatable topics* are topics that have two sides and allow people to choose one side or the other (Example: A professional athlete who tests positive for steroids should lose the right to participate in that sport).

Once the student topics have been submitted, compile a class list of topics that one would assume are debatable. To determine which topics are truly debatable, read each topic to the class, and ask students to determine whether they agree or disagree. An even division of students who agree and students who disagree makes a perfect topic for whole-class debates. Conversely, a 75% to 25% distribution on a topic means that it should be excluded from whole-class debates.

Activity2: Whole-Class Debates

Divide the classroom so that an equal number of desks are on each side of the room. Desks should be facing the middle of the room with a space dividing the two sides. Review the following guidelines for whole-class debates:

- Be courteous to fellow students.
- Listen to the comments and questions of every student.
- Do not speak while other students are speaking.
- Raise your hand and be recognized by the teacher before speaking (unless a question is specifically directed to you).
- If you change your opinion at any time during the debate, simply stand up, move to the other side of the room, and be seated. Be prepared to explain your change in opinion.

Continue each discussion until ideas have been exhausted or until students lose interest. This activity is designed to help students learn how arguments should be formulated by listening to the arguments and responses of their peers. Once students feel comfortable formulating arguments, they are prepared to move on to small group debates.

Activity 3: Small-Group Debates

To prepare for small-group debates, divide students into groups of two or three. Have each group debate a topic against another group. A simple and fair way to assign debates is to place slips of paper with two sides to every topic into a hat and allow students to pick randomly from the hat. For example, one group will pick a slip of paper that reads "(PRO) Evolutionary theories should be taught in public schools," and another will pick a slip that reads "(CON) Evolutionary theories should not be taught in public schools." These two groups would debate against each other and argue the position exactly as it is stated on their slip of paper.

Each group will prepare an opening speech, a list of questions to ask the opposition, possible counter-arguments to their position, and a closing speech. Each debate assumes the following format:

1. Moderator (teacher) announces position to be debated

2. PRO debater presents position (5 minutes)

3. Question and answer period (questions by CON) (3 minutes)

4. CON debater presents position (5 minutes)

5. Question and answer period (questions by PRO) (3 minutes)

6. PRO rebuttal (responses to arguments raised) (3 minutes)

7. CON rebuttal (responses to arguments raised) (3 minutes)

8. PRO debater sums up position (3 minutes)

9. CON debater sums up position (3 minutes)

Each team must research its topic to produce an effective argument. Each argument should be supported by evidence and examples obtained as a result of their research. Research must include at least

- Two Internet references
- Three articles from periodicals (found in *Reader's Guide to Periodical Literature*)
- Two references from other sources (books, newspapers, news media, etc.)

Students prepare and submit a packet that includes all materials needed for the debate. The packet includes the following:

- Cover page
- List of points that support their argument
- List of points that support their opponents' argument
- Opening speech
- Questions to ask opponents
- Closing argument
- Works referenced sheet

Helpful Tips

This lesson can be adapted to fit different grade levels and students with differing abilities. The following list provides insight into the many extensions that may arise as a result of the lesson:

- Address social skills in classes where orderly argumentation issues arise. Teachers can use this lesson to teach students how to respect the opinions of others and to consider multiple viewpoints.
- Address the validity of resources in classes where questionable Internet or periodical references are used.
- Introduce students to the *Reader's Guide to Periodical Literature* as a reference source. Many students are unaware of sources other than the Internet for research.

(Continued)

(Continued)

- Support students in their efforts to complete a task-oriented assignment that requires collaboration with peers and a cooperative effort.
- Instruct students about the proper ways to cite references using the APA or MLA style formats.
- Define plagiarism and its consequences.
- Use this lesson as a springboard for and introduction to persuasive essays or research papers. Students are now familiar with research techniques, logical arguments, and effective support and will be prepared for extensions in these areas.
- Allow students to create ownership of the lesson. They begin by choosing topics that are important to them and continue by developing ideas of their own to consider and support. This creates a meaningful learning experience.

29. Discoveries in Hemingway's "A Clean Well Lighted Place"

Elizabeth G. Lutz-Hackett
Yellow Springs, Ohio

Recommended Level: Grades 10–12

Overall Objective: Students will use reading strategies to comprehend and analyze Ernest Hemingway's "A Clean Well Lighted Place," specifically in regard to the use of imagery and characterization.

Standards Met: Evaluate the author's use of point of view in a literary text; Compare and contrast motivations and reactions of literary characters confronting similar conflicts (e.g., individual vs. nature, freedom vs. responsibility, individual vs. society), using specific example of characters' thoughts, words, and actions; Explain ways characters confront similar situations and conflict; Apply reading comprehension strategies, including making predictions, comparing and contrasting, recalling and summarizing, and making inferences and drawing conclusions.

Materials Needed:

- Markers or colored pencils
- Edward Hopper painting *Nighthawks* (print or computer image)

- Projector with document camera, or computer, or overhead
- Copies of Ernest Hemingway's "A Clean Well Lighted Place"

In this study of Ernest Hemingway's "A Clean Well Lighted Place," students begin by brainstorming on the imagery of light and dark. Later, the students refer back to their brainstorm and relate the connotations to the imagery in the story. Also, before reading the story, students view and write about Edward Hopper's painting, *Nighthawks,* which was inspired by Hemingway's writing. Students will then read the story and follow with a character worksheet to explore the comparison of the young waiter and the old waiter. The lesson culminates with a discussion of Erik Erikson's theory of human development and how it can be applied to the story.

Activity 1: Brainstorm Light and Dark Imagery

- On the left side of a paper, ask students to brainstorm ideas related to the word *light.* Students may write concrete ideas, abstract ideas, images, or connotations.
- Have the students share their ideas "popcorn style."
- On the right side of the paper, ask students to brainstorm ideas related to the word *dark.* Students may write concrete ideas, abstract ideas, images, or connotations.
- Have the students share their ideas popcorn style.
- Ask students to remember the images brainstormed when they read Hemingway's short story.

Activity 2: View Hopper Painting

- Show the students a copy of the painting *Nighthawks* by Edward Hopper.
- On a piece of paper divided into two columns (or on a prepared handout), have the students write in the left column facts about the painting—things they can *actually* see in the painting. They should not hypothesize at this point.
- Have the students share facts they recorded about the painting.
- In the right column, have the students write ideas they have about the painting. Who are these people? What time of day is it? Why are they in the diner? What is the story?
- Ask the students to share their ideas.
- Tell the students that the Hemingway story and the painting have much in common and to remember some of their ideas as they read.

Activity 3: Read Hemingway's "A Clean Well Lighted Place"

- Read the story aloud.

Activity 4: Explore Characterization of the Waiters

- In the left column of a paper, ask the students to write ideas about the young waiter, including words that capture the character's traits, textual quotes related to the character, and essential words from the text.
- In the right column of the paper, have the students write ideas about the old waiter, including words that capture the character's traits, textual quotes related to the character, and essential words from the text.
- Tell the students that they may also include images and drawings about each character.
- Conduct a whole-class discussion about the characterization of each waiter using the ideas from the students' papers.
- During the discussion, ask the students to draw on the ideas they discovered in the prereading activities.

Activity 5: Erik Erikson's Stages of Development

- Prepare a two-column worksheet for the study of Erik Erikson's (1980) stages of development. In the left column list his Eight Stages of Man:

  1. Trust versus Mistrust

  2. Autonomy (self-rule or self-government) versus Shame and Doubt

  3. Initiative versus Guilt

  4. Industry versus Inferiority

  5. Identity versus Role Confusion

  6. Intimacy versus Isolation

  7. Generativity versus Stagnation

  8. Integrity versus Despair

- Provide notes on each stage for the students to record.
- In the right column, headed "Examples of Stage," have the students add appropriate examples
- Conduct a whole-class discussion based on the following questions:

  What stage is the young waiter in? Why?

  What stage is the old waiter in? Why

  What stage is the old man in? Why?

HelpfulTips

- "A Clean Well Lighted Place" is a sophisticated story, so the teacher should continually help the students with the literary ideas. The prereading strategies will help students notice imagery in the story; however, the teacher should support students to make those connections.

(Continued)

(Continued)

- Hemingway does not make clear who is speaking in the story. I often have several readers each take a different role, including the narrator. This helps cut down on confusion.
- This lesson can be adapted to many levels because of the supportive reading strategies that are included. Advanced students should be pushed during discussion. Lower-level students should be given more teacher support.
- Teachers will need to become familiar with Erik Erikson's (1980) Eight Stages of Man to complete the lesson.
- The lesson can also culminate with a written response or a creative writing piece that uses the style of Hemingway.

Reference

Erikson, E. H. (1980). *Identity and the life cycle*. New York: Norton.

Teaching
Social Studies

Overview, Chapters 30–35

30. **Gretchen Smith,** a social studies teacher in Hagerstown, Maryland, enables students to develop an understanding of how historians piece together history by having them create artifacts and use them to draw conclusions about the past. The lesson is a great way to begin a history course and to capture students' interest and engagement from the beginning

31. **Justin G. Singleton,** a geography teacher in Houston, Texas, engages his students in researching various African countries' political, economic, historical, geographic, and social data. They compare and contrast these countries by creating a "lunch sack" that includes all their country's information and having a "class picnic" to share their research.

32. **Terry Armstrong,** a social studies teacher in Warren, Ohio, developed a lesson that offers students an opportunity to take part in a simulated caucus that includes candidates from a major party. The students learn about the difference between a primary vote and a caucus.

33. **Terry Armstrong,** in a second lesson, incorporates a new twist into the standard class review game in preparation of an upcoming examination. The class is divided into two teams, and upon getting a question correct, a team draws a state card and receives a point total equal to the number of electoral college votes the selected state has. First team to reach 270 points wins.

34. **Kristen S. McDaniel,** an economics teacher in Fort Atkinson, Wisconsin, offers a lesson in which students use the city where their high school is located to analyze businesses in the area based on business types (such as sole proprietorship, corporation, and nonprofit) and market types (such as monopolistic competition, oligopoly, and monopoly).

35. **Ann E. Scharfenberg,** an economics teacher in New Richmond, Wisconsin, has students participate in an in-class simulation that enables them to recognize that resources are not evenly distributed, wealth is created if comparative advantage and specialization occurs, and jobs are outsourced.

℞ 30. Piecing Together the Past: An Introduction to the Study of History

Gretchen Smith
Hagerstown, Maryland

Recommended Level: Grades 9–12

Overall Objective: Students will be able to analyze an artifact to determine what information it can provide about the past, examine the differences between historical fact and interpretation, and evaluate the impact of their own bias on analyzing artifacts.

Materials Needed:

- Terra cotta pots or Grecian urn handout
- Paint and paintbrushes or markers and colored pencils
- Plastic bags (large enough to hold broken pots) or envelopes
- Glue or tape
- Scissors
- Sheet or drop cloth (optional)

This activity provides a creative way to begin any study of history. Students create an artifact modeled on the pottery of ancient Greece.

The artifact they create is a visual representation of their own lives, giving peers and the teacher the opportunity to learn more about each other. Students break apart their creations, which are redistributed, giving the students the opportunity to analyze the significance of artifacts as historical evidence and guess who the artist is. By analyzing the pottery, students learn about the importance of artifacts and interpretation in the study of history. You can extend the lesson by leading discussions about the nature of historical evidence and the significance of examining perspectives and bias when studying history.

Activity 1: What Is History?

On a sheet of paper, ask students to list words that come to mind when you say "history." After allowing students time to think, go around the room and have each student give you a response. Compile a list of student responses. Discuss student responses. Ask questions such as the following:

- What do these terms have in common?
- How do people feel about history?
- How do these responses reflect what you expect to get out of this class?

Activity 2: Creating an Artifact

This activity has two variations.

Variation 1: Creating an artifact from a terra cotta pot

Provide each student with a terra cotta pot, paintbrush, paint, water, and cleanup materials. Direct students as follows: On the pot, you must paint at least five pictures to represent different aspects of your life or personality. Do not put your name on the pot. Read the list below for some suggestions about what to paint:

- Favorite color
- Favorite food

- Favorite place to visit
- Favorite sport or team
- Favorite subject
- Favorite ice cream
- Your family
- Favorite music
- Hobbies

Variation 2: Creating an artifact on paper

Provide each student with an outline of a Grecian urn (such as that shown in Figure 30.1) and markers or colored pencils. Follow the instructions from Variation 1, but have the students draw as opposed to paint.

Activity 3: Analyzing Pieces of the Past

Variation 1: Analyzing clay pots

- Take students outside and have them drop their pots one by one. (I put a sheet down first to make it easy to pick up the pieces.) It may be necessary to drop a pot more than once, but tell students to resist the urge to have many small pieces.
- After each drop, students should place the pieces of their pot in a bag. It is not necessary to have every single piece because archaeologists often don't have every piece of evidence when studying the past.
- Collect and number the bags. Keep a record for yourself of the numbers of the students' pots.
- Return to the classroom, and give each student a bag that is not his or her own. Have students piece the assigned pot together as best they can. On a sheet of paper have students write the pot number assigned to them and answer the following questions:

  1. What are the pictures of?

  2. What do the pictures represent or mean?

  3. Describe the person who owned the object based on what you can piece together.

  4. What do you think the object would have been used for? Why?

  5. How does your experience alter your impressions of the artifact?

Figure 30.1 Outline of a Grecian Urn

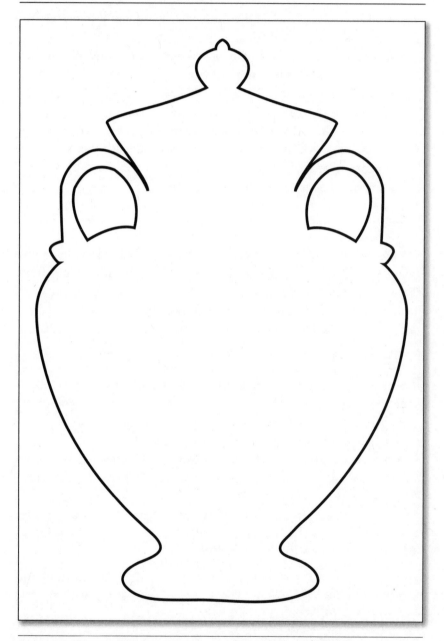

Variation 2: Analyzing paper urns

- Have students cut out their urns and tear them into pieces. You may want to have them select a piece to remove.
- After tearing the urn into pieces, have each student put their pieces in an envelope or plastic bag.
- Collect and number the bags, and keep a record of the numbers and corresponding student names.
- Give each student a bag that is not his or her own. Have the students piece the urn together as best they can. On a sheet of paper have students write the urn number assigned by you and answer the previously listed questions.

Activity 4: Debriefing

Discuss the questions with the students as a class. Use the opportunity to talk with them about where historical evidence comes from, the difference between historical fact and interpretation, and how perspective and memory can affect the interpretation.

Helpful Tips

- I don't typically tell students ahead of time that they will be breaking the pot. Because it will be broken, don't encourage perfection in painting or allow students too much time, as they may be saddened later to break their artwork.
- I have found it difficult sometimes to glue the terra cotta pots back together. You may find it preferable to have students lay out the pieces instead.

---

31. African Lunch Sack and Picnic

Justin G. Singleton
Houston, Texas

Recommended Level: Grades 8–9

Overall Objective: Students will compare and contrast political, economic, geographic, historical, and social information about various African countries.

Standards Met (Texas): The student understands how people, places, and environments have changed over time and the effects of these changes on history; the reasons for the location of economic activities (primary, secondary, tertiary, and quaternary) in different economic systems; the geographic processes that influence political divisions, relationships, and policies; how the components of culture affect the way people live and shape the characteristics of regions; the ways in which cultures change and maintain continuity.

Materials Needed:

- Brown paper bag
- Construction paper
- Markers, scissors, glue
- Internet access
- African Lunch Sack handout for each student
- Country Comparison handout for each student

Conducting research and writing research papers are a common way of accessing student's knowledge of a particular subject. However, students are sometimes intimidated by the research process. This project allows students to utilize those same research skills but also to tap into their creative and artistic side.

Students choose an African country and research its physical, political, economic, and historical geography. Once they have completed their research, they present this research by creating an African Lunch Sack. The students are given brown paper lunch bags to decorate with their country's flag and a map. In the bag, they put information on the country in the form of items commonly found in a lunch sack. Once the lunch sack is constructed, the students participate in a class picnic, in which they share information on their countries. Students complete a comparison chart for the countries that they learn about during the picnic.

Activity 1: Introducing the Research Project

Using the African Sack Lunch handout (see Figure 31.1) as a guide, explain to students the parameters of the research project. You may choose to have students use class time to conduct their research or have them research on their own.

Figure 31.1   Handout for African Lunch Sack Project

Preparing an African Lunch Sack

Overview of the Project

You will research the physical, cultural, historical, and economic issues of a particular African country. As you finish your research, you will prepare an African Lunch Sack as proof that you understand your country. For the project, I will give you a brown paper bag. In this bag, you will put representations of elements of your country: notes on physical characteristics such as rivers, lakes, and mountains; brief history of the country; political geography, such as government type and leader; and economic geography, such as Gross Domestic Product (GDP) and resources. But there is a catch: This isn't just any bag; this is a lunch bag. The items you put in your bag should represent what you eat at lunch (sandwich, drink, chips, candy bar, etc.). For example, just like a sandwich is made up of two pieces of bread and stuff in the middle, your country is also made up of two ends and "stuff" in the middle.

Details of the Project

The following is a list of items you need in or on your bag and what needs to be on or included on each item:

Bag		▪ Country flag ▪ Pictures that illustrate life in the country ▪ Map of the country and map of Africa with you country colored
Sandwich	Bread 1	▪ History of the country (this could be in the form of a timeline)
	Bread 2	▪ Life in the country today! Are there any current issues such as war, hunger, famine, or disease?
	Meat	▪ Economic information: GDP, resources, major imports and exports
	Cheese	▪ Government: type, current leader, and political issues
	Lettuce	▪ Standard of living: life expectancy, literacy rate, urbanization, per capita income
	Tomato	▪ Education: school life

Chips	■ On one side of the chip, create questions about your country that can be answered from the information in your bag. On a separate chip, provide the answer. *(You **MUST** have at least six chips total—three questions and three answers!)*
Drink	■ Physical geography: Provide information on the physical characteristics of your country, such as rivers, lakes, mountains, and so on.
Dessert	■ Information on arts, literature, music, dance, sports, or anything else that would be considered a part of leisure time.

Above and Beyond

- Use a lot of color and decorations when creating the outside of the bag. Make the title large and colorful.
- When creating your items to go in the bag, make them as realistic as possible. You could make your items 3-D, put your chips or your sandwich in a zip-top bag, cover a clean, empty can or milk carton for your drink, add a straw or even a napkin, and so on.
- Create a name for your specific candy bar.
- Above all, have fun and be creative.

Remember: Don't get so caught up in the process that you forget about content. What you write on each item is very important.

Activity 2: Picnic Day

Bring several blankets, or have students bring some of their own. Partner students up and have them sit around the room. In their groups, they are to present their country to their partner. They are to compare country data by filling out the comparison chart shown in Figure 31.2. Have students rotate at least two or three times in order to see several different country projects and add the information to their chart.

Figure 31.2 African Country Comparison Chart

Country Name	Geography	Government/Economics	Interesting Facts	Standard of Living Data

Activity 3: Follow Up Questions

Using the following questions, engage the students in a discussion in which they draw on what they learned:

- Of the three or four countries that you learned about, which country was the least developed?
- Was there anything that your country had in common with the others that you learned about?
- Everyone that had a country that was colonized by France please stand. Britain. Germany. Stand if your country was colonized by a European country that I have not mentioned. What conclusion can you draw? (Students should notice that most countries were colonized by France and Great Britain.)
- Can someone share something interesting about their country that others would not know?
- Everyone line up in front of the class from the country with the largest GDP to the country with the smallest GDP. (You will have to give students time to organize themselves. Maybe have them write the GDP on a sheet of paper and hold it in front of themselves.)

32. Presidential Caucus Simulation

Terry Armstrong
Warren, Ohio

Recommended Level: Grades 10–12

Overall Objective: Students will be prepared to take part in the electoral process as active, educated citizens.

Standards Met (Ohio):

Government: Describe the ways in which public officials are held accountable for the public good, including ways they can acquire and lose their offices—with emphasis on primary and general elections; Identify and analyze issues related to the election process in the United States (e.g., election board policies, technology used in elections, media reporting of election results).

Materials Needed:

- Internet access
- Political handouts (optional)

- Signs for each party candidate
- State party rules for caucuses (if applicable)

What is the difference between a primary and a caucus? What advantage is there to having a caucus rather than a primary? Why do Iowa and New Hampshire get to go first? How does a caucus work? These are all questions we, as government teachers, are asked, particularly around the time of the presidential election. This lesson will provide students with an opportunity to analyze the positions of candidates and take part in a simulated caucus to demonstrate preference for the candidate of their choice.

Preparation

A political party will need to be selected. You may use both for a larger class. Once the party is determined, you should gather information about each of the party's candidates. You may also decide to assign a candidate to each member of the class and require them to create an information sheet about the candidate's stances or a PowerPoint presentation with the same goals.

If you choose to gather the information yourself, you can simply go to each of the candidate's individual Web sites and predetermine the sections you will have students analyze. If you provide print resources about each candidate to students, make certain that consistent issues are addressed in the handouts.

Student Activity: Party Caucus Simulation

The Party Caucus Simulation should take place only after students have had access to quality information about all of the party candidates.

Caucuses are a persuasive event. I find it appropriate after students are finished analyzing candidate positions and experiences that a commercial from each candidate's Web site be used to encourage support. Students should be told that in an actual caucus situation anywhere from dozens to hundreds of people attend and many are trying to persuade you to vote for their candidate. If you have a student or several students who like a particular candidate, it is appropriate to have them try and convince others to support their candidate.

On the day of the caucus, simulation tables should be set up around the room with the candidate names affixed to each one. This will ultimately be where the supporters of that candidate convene. If you have a student that enthusiastically supports a candidate, it would be appropriate to have them at that location. A literature table can also be made available for literature from all party candidates. I have found our county parties to be more than happy to provide literature, and some even provide political signs that can be utilized as the table markers.

A sign-in sheet with the students' name on it will be each student's first stop in the simulation. Students will verify their attendance and that they will be taking part in this party's caucus. Following a predetermined deadline, the rules of the caucus will be read by you or a nonpartisan student: "Our Precinct will be sending one delegate to the National Convention. That delegate will be elected in the following manner." (Caution, state party rules can vary, and you may want to check your state party Web site to get the most up-to-date information regarding delegate selection so you can convey it to the students.) Here are examples of party rules, as adapted for this activity:

- Republican Caucus—A straw vote of those attending the caucus is taken. This vote can be done by a show of hands or by having students go to the tables of the candidate of their choice and then counting them or having them vote on paper ballots.
- Democratic Caucus—Candidates must receive at least 15% of the votes in the precinct caucus to move on to the county convention where delegates to the state convention will be elected. If a candidate receives less than 15% of the votes,

supporters of nonviable candidates have the option to join a viable candidate group, join another nonviable candidate group to become viable, join other groups to form an uncommitted group, or go nowhere and not be counted. Nonviable groups have up to 30 minutes to realign; if they fail to do so in time, they can ask for more time (this might be difficult in a traditional one period class), which would be voted on by the entire caucus. If no additional time is provided, re-alignment is completed, and delegates to the county convention are rewarded.

The Democratic Caucus could result in a considerable amount of "arm twisting." You will need to be part of facilitating the process from beginning to end to make all students feel safe about their choice.

Helpful Tips

- This lesson is best used during a unit on political participation and the role of political parties.
- Students should have prior understanding of the two major political parties.
- Students should be exposed to the role of the delegate in the presidential nominee process. A distinction will have to be made between the rules of the Democrats and Republicans in regard to delegates, specifically in regard to the Republican emphasis on a winner-take-all system and the Democrats' system of proportional allocation. Textbook resources, PowerPoint presentations, or Internet resources of each major party could be utilized in providing students with this understanding.
- I suggest doing caucuses for both parties. Not only will this be more unbiased to the observer and participant, it will also demonstrate a true contrast in caucus rules.
- If this activity is done early in the election process, the media may want to observe the students taking part in the process.

33. Electoral College Review Game

Terry Armstrong
Warren, Ohio

Recommended Level: Grades 9–12

Overall Objective: Students prepare for an upcoming assessment while reinforcing their knowledge of the manner in which the United States elects its president.

Standards Met (Ohio):

Government: Describe the ways in which public officials are held accountable for the public good, including ways they can acquire and lose their offices with emphasis on the electoral college.

Materials Needed:

- Electoral College Flash Cards—available at the following link to C-Span's Web site http://www.c-spanclassroom.org/PDF/fla shcards.pdf
- Electoral college map of the United States
- Review questions for a unit or chapter for which students are preparing for an assessment
- Whiteboard or interactive whiteboard to keep track of each team's electoral college vote total
- Copy of the U.S. Constitution—available at http://www.usconstitution .net/consttop_elec.html
- Copy of Federalist Paper 63—available at http://avalon.law.yale.edu/ 18th_century/fed68.asp

The race for the U.S. presidency has captivated the nation since the close margin of five electoral college votes in the year 2000 followed by a close margin in 2004 and what looked to be another close race in 2008. The nightly news and 24-hour cable news networks cover the presidential race as a horse race, with daily tracking polls in every state described and calculated to come up with a projected winner. Despite the renewed interest in the process, many do not understand the constitutional intent of this system and the manner in which it works.

Preparation

Alexander Hamilton's Federalist Paper 68 provides the original argument for the electoral college. Article 2, Section 1 of the U.S. Constitution and the Twelfth Amendment provide students with the context for the authority vested in the electoral college. The availability of the Federalist Papers and U.S. Constitution can provide an excellent opportunity to differentiate instruction in the government classroom. The documents can provide an opportunity for deep analysis by students.

Students will also benefit from seeing the history of the electoral college. An excellent Web resource for this is the site http://www.270towin.com, which provides an interactive view of every electoral college vote total. Popular vote totals are also available. The site can be manipulated by students as they click on each state. They can change the winner of each state, thus changing the electoral college vote allocation. This can be done with the click of a mouse, and if you are fortunate enough to have an interactive whiteboard, students can do this from the whiteboard. If a presidential election is ongoing, students can change state results according to the most current polling (available through http://realclearpolitics.com).

Students gain interest when they see how close the popular votes in some states have been historically. Many are troubled by the electoral college vote allocation by state. They do not feel that states such as California deserve the power they have, while states such as Ohio continue to lose power in this system. This lesson also provides an opportunity to discuss the census, redistricting, and gerrymandering.

Playing the Electoral College Game

Once a proper foundation has been established, and this will vary according to the subject being taught, the game can be implemented to reinforce the understanding of the electoral college. It works best in preparation for a chapter, unit, or semester exam. This will provide the proper amount of questions for students to try to answer during the game. Students should be split up into two teams. In government class, we have used the Federalists versus the Anti-Federalists, but you can let the teams name themselves or assign them names you feel are appropriate.

The team names should be placed on the board. It is best that you ask the questions so that all students take part in the game. You should have all of the questions in hand and begin by asking the first team their first question. You can use any format you wish to determine which team goes first. If the team gets the first question correct, a card with the name of a state (and the electoral vote total if the C-Span cards are used) is randomly and blindly drawn by a student or the teacher. The number of electoral college votes that corresponds with the state will be awarded to the team that got the question correct. If a team misses their question, the other team may steal and try to answer the question. As with the presidency, the first team to 270 wins. You may not get that far due to incorrect answers or a shortened game. You should set up rules in advance and make the rules clear as to who wins and any variations that could take place due to time and the number of questions.

Students typically get very competitive and, as you would expect, are excited to have Florida drawn and disappointed when they get Wyoming. This review game format could result in the team that had the most correct answers losing, but that can be a valuable lesson in the electoral college in itself.

Helpful Tip

Prior to utilizing the electoral college review game for the first time, discuss the constitutional aspect of the system and its application. This takes place more naturally in a government class that is studying these subjects as part of the regular curriculum. Time should be allotted to go over these facets in other social studies classes to prepare students so that they understand the electoral college system.

℞ 34. Economics in My Hometown

Kristen S. McDaniel
Fort Atkinson, Wisconsin

Recommended Level: Grades 11–12

Overall Objective: Students will explain the differences between and give examples of the main business and market types.

Standards Met (National Council for the Social Studies):

Allocation of Goods and Services: Students will compare the benefits and costs of different allocation methods in order to choose the method that is most appropriate for some specific problem and can result in more effective allocations and a more effective overall allocation system.

The Role of Competition: Students will understand that the level of competition in an industry is affected by the ease with which new producers can enter the industry and by consumers' information about the availability, price, and quantity of substitute goods and services.[1]

Materials Needed:

- Overhead machine
- Map of your local area, zoomed in as much as you need to show the general area. An online map site such as Google map is a great place to start. You'll need multiple copies (nine per class), plus an overhead copy of the map.

We all know that students learn best when we allow them to tie the important concepts of our class to something they already know. This economics lesson has students analyze the place they know best: the city in which their high school is located. Before class, this lesson does require some preparation:

You need some basic information to give the students about market types. They need to understand the difference between perfect competitors, monopolistic competitors, oligopolists, and monopolists. They should have a good idea of how many sellers are in each market, how much competition is allowed, and a good base in examples for each (see Figure 34.1 for assistance). Prepare an overhead, PowerPoint, board notes, lecture, discussion, or reading for students to get the basic information.

Figure 34.1   Information on Market Types

Market Type	Number of Sellers	Competition	Type of Product	Examples in Real Life
Perfect competition	Many	Free competition	Identical	Agricultural products
Monopolistic competition	Many	Free competition	Differentiated	Fast food
Oligopoly	Few	Extremely competitive	Identical or differentiated	Domestic automakers
Monopoly	One	No competition	Only one of its kind	Electricity providers

Students also need basic information on business types. They need to know the difference between sole proprietorship, partnership, corporation, franchise, and non-profit businesses. Prepare an overhead, Powerpoint, board notes, lecture, discussion, or reading for students to get the basic information.

You need a decent copy of a map of your area. I like using an online map service because you can print a map on an 8½ × 11 inch sheet right away, so you don't have to mess around with the sizing on a copy machine. Make nine copies of the map per class. You also need to make a plastic copy that can go on an overhead so students can see the entire map at one time. On the plastic copy, mark out eight or nine areas of the city, each of which has at least ten businesses. Use different colors for each region so that you can say, for example, "choose the red area." Don't worry about mixing up market and business types in each area; it would be very difficult to get a perfect representation in any city. On each of the students' copies of the map, outline one of the regions in the color you chose. Be careful to outline the specific area, down to the exact same road.

With that, you are ready for class. This lesson takes approximately three days from start to finish.

Activity 1

Students learn the basic information on market types. Since this can be confusing at times, and they have probably never heard it before, sometimes it's easier to give them this information by straight direct instruction.

Activity 2

Present the map of the city on the overhead. Since you have already marked the areas of the city, students will probably immediately begin talking about which area they want, since having it presented in such a manner is a hint that they will be doing something with it.

Explain to students that they will be analyzing their local area in terms of the market types they just learned about. Go through the map area by area so they understand what businesses are in each area.

Break students into groups of three to five. Randomly choose a group to start. Because this can get very competitive, I usually have my grade book open and have a student choose a number between one and ____, with the last number being however many kids are in the class. Whatever student is next to the number chosen is the one that gets to choose an area of town first. That student chooses another number, and so on.

As they pick, give them the map with the color they chose already outlined on the sheet. This gives them a concrete outline of the boundaries in which they need to stay.

Then, give the groups time to list 10 businesses in their chosen area and start to determine the market types. You should walk around the room to help them figure out those markets. It is often difficult for students to realize that it is extremely rare to see perfect competition in real life. It is also difficult for them to see the difference between monopolistic competition and oligopoly (for this, I usually ask them if the business actively stops other companies from competing against them by putting them out of business or buying them out—in which case, it would be an oligopoly; if not, it is a monopolistic competitor).

Activity 3

Students learn the basic information on business types, distinguishing between sole proprietorship, partnership, corporation, franchise, and nonprofit.

Activity 4

Students return to their list of businesses in the part of town they chose and determine business types for their list.

Activity 5

Finally, students choose one business from their area and make a visual aid for a presentation to the class. The presentation should consist of naming one of the businesses, the market type it falls into and why, and the business type it falls into and why. A visual helps those visual learners who may still be confused. Hearing this information from many different parts of town helps cement the information for students, and it gives them concrete examples from around their community. Presentations are usually only a few minutes long, and students answer any questions from their peers regarding why they chose a certain market or business type.

HelpfulTips

- Make sure you know the majority of businesses in your city's areas. You need to choose areas that have at least 10 businesses each, so if you don't live in the school community, drive around a little bit before you outline the areas on the map.
- Have the maps done completely before the students arrive to class!

Note

1. Copyright © National Council for the Social Studies. Reprinted with permission.

35. Do What You Do Best and Trade for the Rest

Ann E. Scharfenberg
New Richmond, Wisconsin

Recommended Level: Grades 8–12

Overall Objective: Students will be able to define specialization; describe how nations benefit from comparative advantage and free trade; identify three specific goods that could be produced in the United States but would be very costly, and explain in terms of opportunity costs; calculate productivity when given data; and identify positive and negative consequences of specialization.

Standards Met: Free trade increases worldwide material standards of living; Labor productivity is output per worker; Like trade among individuals within one country, international trade promotes specialization and division of labor and increases output and consumption; As a result of growing international economic interdependence, economic conditions and policies in one nation increasingly affect economic conditions and policies in other nations; Two factors that prompt international trade are international differences in the availability of productive resources and differences in relative prices.

Materials Needed:

- Resources: 10 rulers, 10 protractors, 10 compasses, or one per student
- Three manila envelopes to hold resources; one envelope per group
- Worksheet 1 (one copy for each group)
- Worksheet 2 (one copy for each student not participating in Round 2, or 12 per class)
- Worksheet 3 (one copy for each student)
- Scratch paper for each group (five sheets per student)
- Timer
- Overhead projector with markers and transparencies

In this lesson, students participate in a 60-minute simulation that allows them to experience comparative advantage. They create lines, angles, and circles with resources that are provided. Students identify the activity to which their resources are best suited and specialize in one specific activity. At the end of the simulation, students recognize that resources are not evenly distributed, wealth is created if comparative advantage and specialization occurs, and jobs are outsourced.

Preparation

Before class, organize resources into three envelopes: All rulers in one envelope, all compasses in another envelope, and all protractors in the third envelope. Add Worksheet 1 to each envelope. Arrange desks into three groups for students to work together during the activity. It is not necessary to have an equal number of students in each group. Each group receives an envelope containing all the same resources. Have an area set up for students that become unemployed.

Round 1

1. Begin class by asking students to share what they know about globalization. Display the following quote: "Globalization is a process of interaction and integration among the people, companies, and governments of different nations, a process driven by international trade and investment and aided by information technology." (http://www.globalization101.org/ What_is_Globalization.html)

2. Distribute one envelope of resources, Worksheet 1 (see Figure 35.1), and scratch paper to each group. Display and explain the rules for Geometric Design Round 1 (see Figure 35.2). Instruct the students to organize in their groups, sign all members' names on Worksheet 1, and distribute one resource from the envelope to each student to use during Round 1.

Figure 35.1 Worksheet 1 (Sample template—expand to include space for all group members' names)

Record the names of group members, and note the assigned task for Round 1. At the end of the round, the Geometric Design inspector will record the number of acceptable products for each worker. After inspection, total group production and calculate group productivity (total number of products/total number of workers).

Name	Round 1	Production	Round 2	Production
	Lines Angles Circles		Lines Angles Circles	
	Lines Angles Circles		Lines Angles Circles	
	Total # of lines	Output divided by Input	Total # of lines	Output divided by Input
	Total # of angles	Output divided by Input	Total # of angles	Output divided by Input
	Total # of circles	Output divided by Input	Total # of circles	Output divided by Input

Figure 35.2   Geometric Design Rules for Round 1

---

1. The round will be three minutes long.

2. Using the resources in its envelope, each group member must produce only three products: one perfect 10-cm line, one perfect 30-degree angle, one perfect 3-inch circle.

3. A group CANNOT trade, borrow, buy, or take resources from another group. Only resources from its own envelope may be used.

4. All of the items produced will be inspected by the buyer of Geometric Design. The buyer will accept only those items that meet the standards. Only those items accepted by Geometric Design will be counted.

5. A bonus will be awarded to any group that meets the goal of 10 perfect 10-cm lines, 10 perfect 30-degree angles, and 10 perfect 3-inch circles.

---

3. Work time is three minutes for Round 1. After the round is completed, you play the role of the buyers of Geometric Design and inspect all lines, angles, and circles produced. Students record results from your inspection on Worksheet 1.

4. After all groups are inspected, record the group results on the chart shown in Figure 35.3. Debrief Round 1.

   a. Was the task of 10 lines, 10 angles, and 10 circles too difficult given the number of people in each group? *No, there were enough workers, but the resources weren't divided appropriately.*

   b. Why didn't any groups succeed and earn the bonus? *Answers will vary and may include wrong resources, resources were unfairly divided, time too short, and so on.*

   c. If the lines, angles, circles represent production of the basics for survival, food, clothing, and shelter, what would have happened to the groups? *If production levels weren't met, groups wouldn't have survived.*

   d. What are some strategies for changing the activity so that the groups could make enough lines, angles, and circles?

Figure 35.3 Round 1 Results

Geometric Design	Lines	Angles	Circles	Productivity (output/input)
Group A				
Group B				
Group C				
Total				

Answers may include trading resources—good idea but some resources, like oil, aren't mobile; trading people/workers—good idea but workers don't like being told where to live and work. Correct answer: trading products!

Round 2

5. Display the rules for Geometric Design Round 2 (see Figure 35.4). Note that the rules are the same EXCEPT each group is going to use its resources for the task for which they are best suited. That is, the group with the rulers should make lines and only lines, the group with compasses should make only circles, and the group with the protractors should make only angles.

Figure 35.4   Geometric Design Rules for Round 2

1. The round will be 3 minutes long.

2. Using the resources in its envelope, each group must produce only one kind of product—depending on its resource, either perfect 10 cm lines, perfect 30 degree angles, or perfect 3 inch circles

3. A group CANNOT trade, borrow, buy, or take resources from another group. Only resources from its own envelope may be used.

4. All of the items produced will be inspected by the buyer of Geometric Design. The buyer will accept only those items that meet the standards. Only those items accepted by Geometric Design will be counted.

5. A bonus will be awarded to any group that meets the following goals: rulers = 30 perfect lines; protractors = 30 perfect angles; compasses = 30 perfect circles.

Incentive: How many products can your group make? The more products = the greater wealth created.

a. Review Worksheet 1 for each group. Dismiss any student in the group with rulers who didn't make lines in Round 1, saying, "Thanks for your hard work, but this group is not going to need your skills anymore. Sorry, but you are unemployed." Have the students move out of the group to a designated area for Round 2. Repeat the process for each group.

b. Add an incentive for the most productive group within a specified time period or if productivity meets specific targets such as 60 lines/member, 15 angles/member, or 25 circles/member.

c. Unemployed students will have the 3 minute Round 2 to brainstorm ideas for finding employment and record them on Worksheet 2 (see Figure 35.5).

6. Conduct Round 2 for three minutes. After the round is complete, inspect all lines, angles, and circles produced, and record the results for each student on Worksheet 1. After all groups are inspected, record group results on the chart shown in Figure 35.6. Invite the unemployed students to share ideas they brainstormed for becoming employed in the activity.

Analysis of the Simulation

7. Distribute Worksheet 3 to each student (see Figure 35.7). Complete the table. Answers will vary, demonstrating calculations of productivity (number of products produced divided by number of workers—output/input). Students should work together, discussing answers in their respective groups.

8. Closure. Display the following quote from Kofi Annan (U.N. Secretary General, 1997–2006): "It has been said that arguing against globalization is like arguing against the laws of gravity." Discuss with the students globalization, the meaning of the quote, and the implications for trying to stop the forces of globalization. Ask them to consider what this means for them and their future.

Figure 35.5   Worksheet 2—Unemployment Line

Name:

1. Skill: I made _____ during Round 1.

2. Resource of your group (circle one):
   rulers   protractors   compasses

3. Why were you fired?

4. Analyze solutions to finding employment:

Solution	Cost	Benefit
1. Learn new skill		
2. Relocate to new group		
3.		

5. Predict whether your former group will make 30+ products during Round 2?

6. If they do, they will receive a bonus. How do you feel about their success?

7. If they received a reward, is it fair that you are left out?

8. In which round(s) were you satisfied or happy?

9. Should the government make a rule to protect your job and limit trade?

10. What lesson(s) did you learn during this activity?

Figure 35.6 Round 2 Results

Geometric Design	Lines	Angles	Circles	Productivity (output/input)
Group A				
Group B				
Group C				
Total				

Figure 35.7　Worksheet 3

With your group, discuss your experiences of participating in the Geometric Design simulation. Complete the table below.

Geometric Design	Lines		Angles		Circles		Productivity (output/input)	
Group A								
Group B								
Group C								
Total Output								

Individually, write the answers to the following questions.

1. Compare Round 1 to Round 2. What was similar? *Lines, angles, circles were produced, round is 3 minutes in length, resources weren't shared.* What was different? *In Round 2 all groups achieved the bonus, some people lost their jobs, output was greater, and productivity was greater.*

2. What happened to production in Round 2 when the groups specialized? *Production increased, greater productivity.*

3. Which group has a comparative advantage in lines? Identify opportunity costs. *Group with rulers; give up making circles and angles.*

4. Which group has a comparative advantage in angles? Identify opportunity costs. *Group with protractors; give up making lines and circles*

5. Which group has a comparative advantage in circles? Identify opportunity costs. *Group with compasses; give up making lines and angles*

6. List and explain how nations vary in resource availability.

   Land—oil, timber; climate, which may be best suited for certain crops

   Labor—some nations have better skills and education levels (quality), while other nations have greater numbers of people (quantity)

   Capital—technology, access to computers, Internet; tools, equipment, and machines

7. Define comparative advantage. *Comparative advantage is the ability of a person or country to produce a particular good at a lower cost than another person or country.*

(Continued)

Figure 35.7 (Continued)

8. Identify consequences of specialization. *Positive includes increased production, lower prices, and better quality products with increased competition, wealth created, efficient use of resources, greater variety of goods, positive foreign relations. Negative includes unemployment, dependence on other groups, national security issues, and different levels of compliance to standards.*

9. Summarize why businesses and people of different nations trade. *Answers will vary but "if you do what you do best and trade for the rest," people/businesses will benefit with greater income, variety of products, more leisure time. When individuals, regions, and nations specialize in what they can produce at the lowest cost and then trade with others, both production and consumption increase.*

Helpful Tips

■ Have a student be a helper during the activity. They can monitor the time, recycle used paper after rounds, and make sure there is enough paper for Round 2.

■ During Round 2, have students count products as they are being produced. Since students have the appropriate resources, item should be perfect. This saves on time between Round 2 and reflection on Worksheet 3.

■ If extra credit or other bonuses are awarded as productivity incentives, staple all counted products from each group into a packet. If necessary, products can be verified as accurate.

Extension Ideas

■ Discuss the phrase "Buy American," which was an advertising slogan used by Walmart in the 1990s. Why doesn't Walmart use it anymore? How does one "buy American"? Nike shoes are made in Vietnam. Are they American or not? Toyota Camrys are built in Lexington, Kentucky. Are they American or not?

- Show the video clip "Did You Know? 2.0," available on YouTube or TeacherTube, about the changes technology is making in our lives and the need for 21st century skills.
- Compare and contrast the difference location makes for unemployed workers after Round 1. What would happen to unemployed workers if Groups A, B, and C were businesses in same community? The unemployed workers could apply for jobs at the businesses with extra resources requiring their skill set. What would happen to unemployed workers if Groups A, B, and C were businesses in different states? The unemployed may not know about job openings in other states or may not have an opportunity to relocate. What would happen to unemployed workers if Groups A, B, and C were businesses in different nations? Workers need retraining to have skill sets for employment and alternative skills for job openings in other industries.

PART IV

Teaching Music, Art, and Physical Education

Teaching
Music and Art

Overview, Chapters 36–38

36. **Stan Scott,** a vocal music teacher in Grand Junction, Colorado, gives students specific instructions on how to create and produce unified vowels when singing and provides a guided worksheet for self-practice. The students video record themselves individually for evaluation.

37. **Keith Farnsworth,** an art teacher in Jerome, Idaho, has students examine food paintings by Wayne Thiebaud and use colored plasticine clay to "paint" an item of food, creating a thick impasto look in the same style.

38. **Jill Pinard,** an English teacher in Weare, New Hampshire, follows a unit on American Romantic writers with a study of the Hudson River School painters. Students explore an in-class gallery and then create their own pastels inspired by those paintings.

36. Creating Correct Vowels for Singing

Stan Scott
Grand Junction, Colorado

Recommended Level: Grades 7–12

Overall Objective: Students will achieve correct and consistent vowel formation for blending voices in a choir.

Standards Met (Music Educators): Students will create music; Evaluate music and musical performance[1]

Materials Needed:

- Vowel Formation handout
- Video camera
- Vowel evaluation sheet

Typically, choir directors struggle to ensure that all of their singers are producing a unified vowel sound. Producing a unified vowel helps the choir to blend and avoid pitch problems or a sound that is too strident. By giving all students a Vowel Formation handout, students are provided with a reference sheet to help them achieve correct vowel formation and to give them the tools to know how to correctly form vowels that are used in singing. Having all students produce the exact same vowel will help to produce a better tone from the choir.

Activity 1: Instruction and Practice

Give the students the Vowel Formation handout (see Figure 36.1). Go over each vowel as it is described, and make sure that the students understand how to produce each of the 10 vowels for singing (which are modified from the typical five vowels they study in language classes). On the left-hand side of the handout is a word that corresponds to the vowel sound that the student is supposed to say. All of the words start with the consonant *B* to avoid confusion with the correct vowel sound.

Have the students select a partner and quiz each other to see if they can make the correct vowel formation using the prompts that are given in the "How to produce it" column of the handout. They can help each other to correct discrepancies or ask you questions about producing a correct vowel sound.

Figure 36.1 Vowel Formation: Correct Placement of Vowel Sounds

All vowels should feel lifted and forward (in the cheek bones of the face) and should be supported with a good breath. The soft palate in the back of your throat should be lifted, like when you yawn or bite an apple.

Comparable word	Vowel	How to produce it
1. BEET	"EE"	Teeth one finger wide (open). Tongue relaxed and forward (on the lower front teeth). Corners of the lips in, (not spread) in a natural way.
2. BAIT	"A" (LIKE THE LETTER "A")	Teeth slightly more open than one finger. Tongue relaxed and forward (on the lower front teeth). Corners of the lips in, (not spread) in a natural way.
3. BOX	"AH"	Teeth and mouth should be one and one half fingers wide open. Tongue relaxed and forward (on the lower front teeth). Corners of the lips in (not spread) in a natural way. Inside smile.
4. BOAT	"OH"	Rounded lips but open, and mouth should be one and one half fingers wide open. Tongue relaxed and forward (on the lower front teeth). Inside smile.
5. BOOT	"OO"	Rounded lips, but corners of mouth in, kind of like when you kiss someone, but more open. One finger wide open for teeth. Tongue relaxed and forward (on the lower front teeth).
6. BET	"EH"	Teeth slightly more open than one finger. Tongue relaxed and forward (on the lower front teeth). Corners of the lips in (not spread) in a natural way.

Comparable word	Vowel	How to produce it
7. BOUGHT	"AW"	The sound is between OH and AH. Tongue relaxed and forward (on the lower front teeth). Mouth should be one and half a fingers wide open. Lift the cheek bones or smile on the inside of your mouth.
8. BAT	"aaaaa"	Teeth slightly more open than one finger. Tongue relaxed and forward (on the lower front teeth). Corners of mouth not spread but in a natural position.
9. BUT	"UH"	Teeth slightly more open than one finger (can be used but be careful of the sound). Tongue relaxed and forward (on the lower front teeth). Corners of mouth not spread but in a natural position.
10. BIT	"IH"	One finger wide open for teeth. Tongue relaxed and forward (on the lower front teeth). Corners of mouth not spread, but in a natural position.

Activity 2: Evaluation

After students have practiced producing vowels with a partner, have the students individually go into a room with a video camera to tape themselves doing all 10 of the vowels. So that you can continue with the class, have the students independently rotate through the testing room. As a student finishes videoing, he or she can consult a class list posted on the door to find out who is next on the list and quietly notify that student to proceed to the testing room.

You can later view the video recordings and evaluate the students using the form in Figure 36.2. If a student did not make the correct vowel sound, put a number in the fail column that corresponds to an appropriate item on the list of typical problems. This helps the students

Figure 36.2   Vowel Test Evaluation Form

Name: _____ Grade: _____

Grades, based on number of vowels failed:

0 = A+   4 = C–

1 = A–   5 = D

2 = B   6 = D–

3 = C+

Vowel	Pass	Fail
EE beet		
A(ay) bait		
AH box		
OH boat		
OO boot		
EH bet		
AW bought		
aaaaa bat		
UH but		
IH bit		

Comments:

1. The corners of your mouth are too spread.

2. Your mouth is not open wide enough.

3. You don't have enough space between your upper and lower teeth.

4. It sounds like your tongue is not forward.

5. You didn't say the correct vowel.

6. You didn't do the test correctly! For example, if you were to say the vowel eeee, you were supposed to say the word *beet* and then make the correct vowel sound "eeeeeee" for about two seconds. Then wait two seconds and do the next word with its vowel sound.

to know what they need to correct so that they can pass that vowel when they retake the test. It is a good idea for the students to take the entire test over, not just the vowels that they got wrong. Consistency of vowel production is the goal, and practicing each one over and over perfectly will help them achieve the desired results.

Helpful Tips

- If you decide to test students with a video camera, it is important that students' privacy is respected. If possible, find a room that does not have windows. It is also important to assure the students that only you will be watching the video and that it is only going to be watched for evaluation purposes and helping the students to produce a vowel that is consistent with the rest of the choir. Only one student at a time should test, and students can be shown how to turn the video camera on and off so that it does not have to stay running the entire time.

- If a student is absent the day of the test, remind students that are getting the next student to test that they should skip over the absent student and go to the next person on the list. Including a seating chart or pictures of students with the list is helpful, just in case students do not know each other.

- During the testing, students should be allowed to use the prompts of putting their fingers in their mouth to achieve the correct vowel form, as described on the handout.

- It is beneficial to have the students keep taking the test until they can pass it with at least a 90% or more. It is not unusual to have a student need to retake the test five to six times. It is important that you help the students that are having a problem with opening their mouth to make the correct vowel sounds.

- Students must be reminded that singing in a choir is not like regular talking. Choral singing is more open and requires more space between the upper and lower teeth. The benefits will become apparent as the year progresses and you find that you don't have to prompt students to open their mouths wider when they are singing.

Note

1. Adapted from *Colorado Model Content Standards: Music,* by the Colorado Department of Education. Retrieved April 1, 2010, from http://www.cde.state.co.us/cdeassess/documents/OSA/standards/music.pdf

▧   37. Wayne Thiebaud–Style Plasticine Painting

Keith Farnsworth
Jerome, Idaho

Recommended Level: Grades 10–12

Overall Objective: Students will create a Wayne Thiebaud–style painting using colored clay as their medium.

Standards Met: Identify representative visual works of art from a variety of cultures and historical periods; Analyze a visual art product or art performance that integrates media, processes, and/or concepts from other performing arts disciplines; Analyze an artist's use of elements, principles, and how they contribute to one's interpretation of the artwork; Plan and produce a work of art using media, techniques, and processes with skill, confidence, and sensitivity; Create an interpretation of a work respecting the intent of its creator; Create a body of work that develops a specific theme, idea, or style of art.

Materials Needed:

- Variety of colored plasticine clay
- 9 × 12 inch canvas panels
- Modeling tools
- Pencils
- Clear spray varnish
- Magazines with food photos
- Slide show or written text with images depicting Wayne Thiebaud's work.

This project works best with students who have previously taken basic drawing. Students first examine the works of Wayne Thiebaud by viewing his paintings in the February 2003 issue of *Scholastic Art*. Students also read a short biography and brief summary of his work and style in this same issue. If this publication is not available, substitute a slide show of his food paintings and a brief discussion of his life and works with information taken from the Internet. Students then find a photo of a food they would like to paint. They draw the food image on a canvas panel and then apply colored clay to create paintings in the style of Thiebaud. (See samples of student work in Figure 37.1.)

Figure 37.1 Samples of Student Work in the Thiebaud Style

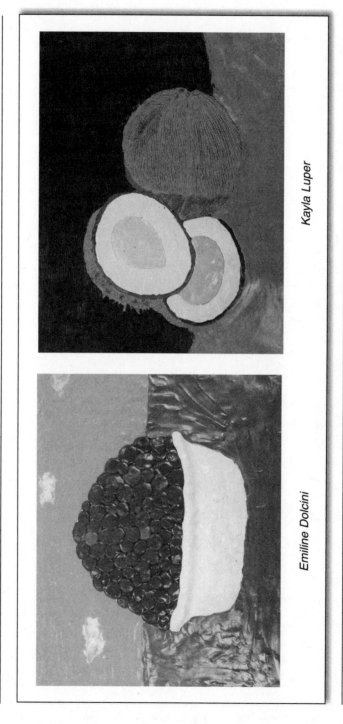

Emiline Dolcini

Kayla Luper

(Continued)

Figure 37.1 (Continued)

Walker Ostler

Dallin Mena

Activity 1: Read or Study Food Paintings of Wayne Thiebaud

- Have students examine paintings of food done by Thiebaud.
- Discuss his use of art elements, including shape, color, paint application, and texture. Emphasize that Thiebaud applies paint with a thick impasto style.
- Discuss composition possibilities, such as symmetrical or asymmetrical, as well as background colors and cast shadows, all working within a single painting.
- Discuss how using colored clay instead of paint will allow for actual texture versus the illusion of texture.

Activity 2: Choose Food Photo and Draw on Canvas Panel

- Have students search through magazines with photos of food.
- Once food photos have been chosen, have the students cut out the image or the whole page to use as a reference.
- Have the students draw the food image on canvas panels with composition concepts in mind.
- After the food image is drawn, tell the students to draw a table or countertop surface so the image isn't floating. Their compositions with a counter top and background shape usually end up looking like a horizon line.

Activity 3: Paint the Food and Background With Colored Clay

- Demonstrate the optimal ways to mix proper colors. Adding a small amount of the darker of two colors and then mixing them in the hand is best. If more color is needed, it is easier to add small amounts at a time than to mix a large amount of a color that may not even be what is desired.
- Instruct the students to apply plasticine clay to their food drawing. Modeling tools should be available to help them create textures as well as a shape for the clay for their food image. The clay can be scored, poked, stippled, or whatever is needed to produce the textures that will give the food image the look of an impasto style similar to that of Thiebaud.

- Explain that the background and countertop clay colors chosen should not take away from the main food image. These are kept simple and are usually of a lighter value.
- Have the students spray several coats of clear gloss on their paintings when they are completed and there will not be any more clay added. The spray will create a protective crust to help prevent damage to the clay.

Helpful Tips

- The demonstration of mixing colors in clay is very important. To save on clay costs, show students how to avoid mixing muddy colors or too much of a color that they will not use because it became too dark too fast.
- Use cans of clear spray from a discount store to help with costs.
- I order the plasticine from regular school discount art supply magazines.

---

38. Art Integration: Enrolling in the Hudson River School to Study American Romanticism

Jill Pinard
Weare, New Hampshire

Recommended Level: Grades 10–12

Overall Objective: Students will apply their study of American Romanticism to help them analyze the paintings of the Hudson River School and solidify their understanding of Romanticism and Transcendentalism.

Standards Met: Comparing stories or other texts to related personal experience, prior knowledge, or to other books; Synthesizing and evaluating information within or across text(s); Using a text structure appropriate to focus/controlling idea or thesis (e.g., purpose, audience, context); Including sufficient details or facts for appropriate depth of information: naming, describing, explaining, comparing, contrasting, or using visual images to support intended purpose.

Materials Needed:

- Posters of Hudson River School paintings (you could also use a PowerPoint presentation)
- Colored pencils
- Music for the gallery (optional—I usually use Vivaldi's "Four Seasons")

- Chalk pastels
- 16 × 20 inch gray construction paper
- Newspapers
- Student handout: 19th Century Literature and Art Essay

American Romanticism is an essential period in any American literature course. By studying the painters of the Hudson River School, my students gain insight into another aspect of American culture, while reinforcing their understanding of an important literary and philosophical movement of the 19th century. This lesson typically spans two 90-minute blocks or the equivalent.

Activity 1: In the Gallery

- Arrange examples of the Hudson River School paintings around the room.
- At the beginning of class, ask the students to walk around and enjoy the gallery for approximately 10 minutes.
- After they have had a chance to enjoy the gallery, distribute a student handout. Then have students revisit the gallery in small

groups to discuss what they observe and to make small sketches (make colored pencils available). (I expect my students to know three of the works well, but they may choose which ones they study.)

■ To guide the study of their chosen paintings, provide questions such as the following:

1. What attitude is conveyed about the subject matter in each painting?

2. How does each painting reflect, represent, and express its time period? (Think about Emerson, Thoreau, and westward expansion.)

3. Does the painting misrepresent its time period? Explain.

4. What do the paintings have in common?

5. Evaluate each painting. Which do you like? Why? Rank them in order from 1 to 5.

■ For each of their chosen paintings, ask the students to record the following:

Title

Painter

Dimensions

Medium

Description

Attitude about subject

Connection to time

Evaluation

■ In the last 15 minutes before the gallery closes, lead the class in a discussion of the common characteristics in the paintings they viewed. Give them some background on the Hudson River School at this time.

- For the next class, ask each student to bring in a photograph of a place in nature that inspires them. Ideally, this would be a place that has personal significance to them, but allow them to look in magazines or online for something that simply appeals to them.

Activity 2: In the Artists' Studio

- If it is possible to work in your school's art room, that would be the ideal situation, but this part of the lesson can be completed in your classroom—just be sure to put down plenty of newspaper. Students will be working with chalk pastels, which are easy to work with even if one is uncomfortable with art, to recreate the picture they have brought in using the characteristics of the Hudson River School.
- Briefly review some characteristics of the Hudson River School paintings, including the use of light, background versus foreground, and the size of humans depicted.
- Quickly model using pastels, pointing out the importance of starting with the background and blending. If the students accumulate a lot of chalk dust as they work, ask them to shake their work over the trash rather than blowing the dust off.
- Spray on a sealant to preserve the work.
- Have the students title their work, type and affix their own credit line, and then mount their pieces.

Activity 3: At the Writer's Desk

- Assign an essay comparing the works of the Romantic writers to those of the Hudson River painters (see the student handout in Figure 38.1).

Figure 38.1   19th Century Literature and Art Essay

The stars awaken a certain reverence, because though always present, they are inaccessible; but all natural objects make a kindred impression, when the mind is open to their influence.

Ralph Waldo Emerson, "Nature," 1863

Instructions

Write an essay in which you compare the works of the Romantic writers we have studied with the works of the Hudson River School painters we have studied. What attitude about nature do these works reveal? Be sure to provide specific examples from what we have read and what we have viewed to support your position. Use the following criteria to assess your work, and revise if necessary.

Assessment

Introductory Paragraph   10

1. Do you have a grabber sentence that makes your reader want to continue?
2. Is the topic introduced clearly? (four to five lead-in sentences)
3. Is the thesis stated?

Body Paragraph (minimum of three) Organization and Structure   20

1. Is the evidence organized in appropriate paragraphs? (one focused idea per paragraph)
2. Is there a logical sequence to the paragraph order?
3. Do topic sentences identify a specific goal and relate it to the thesis statement?
4. Do clincher sentences summarize each paragraph?

Conclusion   10

1. Are key points summarized to validate the thesis statement?
2. Is a related concept for the reader to reapply to human nature stated?

Evidence   50

1. Does evidence from the texts (including artwork) validate the topic sentences?
2. Does the analysis show the reader how to interpret the evidence?
3. Is there appropriate support for the topic sentences and thesis statement?
4. Is there an examination of key evidence?
5. Is there specific evidence (at least two examples per paragraph)?
6. Have you used quotations where appropriate?
7. Are the titles and authors of the works discussed identified?

Sentence Clarity and Style   10

Helpful Tips

- Your art department may have posters of Hudson River School paintings that you can borrow. I keep my eyes peeled for art calendars that I can cut up, laminate, and keep for the various galleries I use in my classes. When I use art from calendars, I make sure the credit line is included or I type it myself and affix it before I laminate. I think it is especially important for students to be aware of the dimensions and medium of the original work. Since this is an activity I do every year, I have purchased a few large posters and inexpensive frames to make my gallery seem a little more real; the students seem to really appreciate these touches.

- If you do not, however, have access to posters, there are plenty of images available online that you could easily put into a PowerPoint or SMART board presentation. I would still expect my students to sketch two or three examples from this kind of presentation, but it might be more practical to have each student sketch the same works.

- I am fortunate to work in a school where we are encouraged to make interdisciplinary connections. I used to be an art phobe, but when I started inviting art teachers into my classroom, they put me at ease. If it is possible to team teach this lesson with an art teacher, it will be a richer experience for all. I have found that after working with an art teacher a few times, I am able to conduct lessons with confidence myself thereafter.

- This lesson can be modified to use with in-class art galleries on any other topic or time period.

Teaching Physical Education

Overview, Chapters 39–40

39. **Carla Thompson,** a physical education and health teacher from Lake Villa, Illinois, has students use the Internet to find weight-training exercises that work specific muscle groups. The students must describe the exercises and draw stick figures to show how they are done, as well as answer reflective questions.

40. **Kathleen Donaldson,** a physical education teacher from Edgewood, Maryland, has students participate in a series of fitness stations in order to develop greater understanding of how various types of exercises and their effort affect heart rate. They record their heart rates throughout the activities and evaluate their experience.

▧ 39. Interactive Muscle Assignment

Carla Thompson
Lake Villa, Illinois

Recommended Level: Grades 9–12

Overall Objective: Students will demonstrate knowledge of muscle groups and how they work together.

Standards Met:

National Association for Sport and Physical Education: Applies movement concepts and principles to the learning and development of motor skills; Identify and apply critical elements to enable the development of movement competence/proficiency.[1]

Illinois: Achieve and maintain a health-enhancing level of physical fitness based upon continued self-evaluation; participate in various types of fitness training programs and describe the characteristics and benefits of each.

Materials Needed:

■ Computers with Internet access

To begin this activity, students decide what goals they have set for personal muscle strength workouts. They then use the Internet to research different weight-training techniques. Students use creative drawing skills, at the basic level, to show the different skills along with a written description, including answering reflective questions. Following are the instructions to students.

Interactive Muscle Assignment

Go to http://www.gopherfitness.com/exercises.html and drag the mouse over a muscle group; then click on that muscle. You will see a list of exercises for that group. Select two different exercises to work that muscle group. Describe in writing the steps involved in the exercise, and draw stick figures that show the exercise. (Do not use the same exercise for more than one muscle group.) The muscle chosen must be the main muscle worked in the exercise. You need to choose three different muscle groups.

At the end of your paper, answer the following questions:

1. Why did you choose these muscle groups?
2. Which exercise would be the most difficult for you to do? Why?
3. Which muscle group would you most like to work on? Why?
4. Explain how there could be exercises that may use more than one group of muscles.
5. Name three exercises that use more than one muscle group.
6. How do these exercises fit into your overall fitness plan?

Note

1. Adapted from *Moving into the Future: National Standards for Physical Education, 2nd Edition,* with permission from the National Association for Sport and Physical Education (NASPE), 1900 Association Drive, Reston, VA 20191-1599.

▧ 40. Aerobic/Anaerobic Fitness Stations

Kathleen Donaldson
Edgewood, Maryland

Recommended Level: Grades 9–12

Overall Objective: Students will make connections between the types of exercises they perform and the effects their effort has on their heart-rate levels.

Standards Met:

Exercise Physiology: Students will demonstrate the ability to use scientific principles to design and participate in a regular, moderate to vigorous physical activity program that contributes to personal health and enhances cognitive and physical performance on a variety of academic, recreational, and life tasks; Evaluate the factors influencing exercise adherence.

Physical Activity: Students will demonstrate the ability to use the principles of exercise physiology, social psychology, and biomechanics to design and adhere to a regular, personalized, purposeful program of physical activity consistent with their health, performance, and fitness goals in order to gain health and cognitive/academic benefits; Assess and analyze individual aerobic capacity/cardio respiratory fitness; Assess and analyze individual muscular strength and muscular endurance.

Materials Needed:

- Jump ropes
- Floor tape for marking dot drill
- Cones (at least four)
- Agility ladder
- Bosu balls (balance and stability balls)
- Aerobic steps
- Signs posted with directions at each of the stations
- Pedometers
- Heart rate monitors
- Reminders to check and record heart rates after each station
- Record sheet for heart rate
- Pencils for each student

In this lesson, students participate in eight different aerobic fitness stations that focus on various health- and skill-related fitness components: cardiovascular endurance, muscular strength and endurance, flexibility, balance, power, speed, and coordination. The stations are designed to increase student heart rates into their target heart-rate zone. While transitioning from three teacher-designated stations, students perform an anaerobic type of activity to "tease" the heart rate. This provides the students with direct feedback as to how aerobic and anaerobic exercises can affect the heart rate.

Before beginning the lesson, have students put on their heart rate monitors (if available) or take their resting heart rate. Hand out the heart rate data recording chart (see Figure 40.1). Have students record their resting heart rate in the appropriate box on the data sheet. If students have not been introduced to the differences between aerobic and anaerobic exercises, ask them to give examples of activities that can be performed for longer periods of time as well as activities that can only be done for short periods of time. Students should begin to recognize that *aerobic* means *with oxygen* and *anaerobic* means *without oxygen.* Ask students to anticipate what might happen to their heart rates if their muscles are not getting enough oxygen to continue working at full effort. Explain that during the fitness stations students participate in activities that focus on both aerobic and anaerobic exercises. It is also important to discuss how an individual's personal effort during exercise affects their heart rate.

Begin a walk-through and explanation of each of the stations. Stations should be set up around the perimeter of the gymnasium with ample space to move. Each station lasts one minute. After one minute of exercise, students check their heart rate levels using a six-second count directed by the teacher, unless students are using heart rate monitors, in which case they look at their monitor and record their heart rate at that time. Transition time between stations should be no more than 10 seconds. The following is a list of suggested activities for eight stations:

1. *A jump-rope activity.* Students should continuously jump rope. If students are struggling with clearing the rope, have them turn the rope on their side while continually jumping. Give the students the choice of the type of jump they would like to perform.

Figure 40.1 Aerobic/Anaerobic Station Record Sheet

Name _____

PD _____

Date	Resting heart rate	Check 1	Check 2	Check 3	Check 4	Check 5	Check 6	Check 7	Check 8	Recovery heart rate after 2 minutes
			anaerobic		anaerobic		anaerobic			
			anaerobic		anaerobic		anaerobic			
			anaerobic		anaerobic		anaerobic			

Answer the following questions:

1. Which stations were most difficult for you? Explain why.

2. How does your individual effort when exercising affect your heart rate?

2. *A cone shuffle slide activity.* Space the cones 10 feet apart. Students start at one cone and shuffle back and forth between two cones. The shuffle slide should be continuous. Remind students to keep their toes pointing forward and not to cross or touch feet as they shuffle.

3. *An agility ladder.* Students are to continuously perform a designated agility exercise inside the ladder (e.g., in/outs, 2 feet in each rung, side steps).

4. *A wall jump exercise.* Students are to continuously jump as high as they can with their arms reaching up above their heads touching the wall. This jump should look similar to a block jump in volleyball. Remind students to stay on the ball of their feet and explode straight up, reaching as high as possible.

5. *A Bosu balance ball drill.* Have the Bosu ball round side facing up (flat side up for more of a challenge). Students are to balance with their eyes closed or open for a count of 10, then sprint to a designated line in the gym (approximately 25 ft. distance) and back to the ball. Repeat the process until time is up.

6. *A cross box jump activity.* The cross box should be laid out on the floor before class begins. The cross box consists of two intersecting lines of tape that look like a large plus sign. The upper left section is number 1, upper right is number 2, lower right is number 3, and the lower left is number 4. Have the students jump in specific numerical orders, for example, 1,2,3,4, or 4,2,3,1. The jumping should be nonstop.

7. *An aerobic step activity.* Students should step in a cadence-like manner with both feet stepping onto, then off of, the box (up right, left; down right, left).

8. *Lunge walks between two sets of cones.* Remind students that while lunge walking, their front knee must stay in line with their front heel and the front leg should reach a 90-degree angle at the knee with their quadriceps parallel to the floor. Also remind them to keep their shoulders to the ceiling and head up.

After the second, fourth, and sixth stations, students engage in a teacher-designated anaerobic exercise for 30 seconds. Pushups, front or side planks, curl ups, wall sits, and squat jumps are examples of activities that have been used during the anaerobic phases of the activity. Have students check and record their heart rates after the anaerobic phases of the station work.

Assign student groups to each station, and begin the station activities. Students should be moving the entire time and should record their heart rates after each station. Some modifications may be made in order to help struggling students complete an exercise. After completing one complete cycle of the stations, have students walk the perimeter of the gym for two minutes. After one minute, have students check their heart rate and continue walking. Students' heart rates should be dropping during the cool-down time. After the second minute, have students take their heart rate again and record the number in the recovery heart rate box on the record sheet.

Bring students together for closure, and address the class objectives. Discuss the trend they noticed in their heart rate levels as well as the type of activities they performed. Question the students about the differences between the aerobic and anaerobic activities. Have them explain how FITT (frequency, intensity, time, and type) was applied to the workout. As a final activity, have students answer the questions at the bottom of the record sheet.

Helpful Tips

- Have signs with pictures and descriptors at each station, along with possible modifications to increase or decrease difficulty.
- Change the time limit at each station as needed.
- If you do not have certain pieces of equipment, add in a different aerobic activity.